GENERATIONAL WEALTH: RICH FROM THE INSIDE OUT

(A complementary piece to the website: seeyourdollar.com)

Written by:
Gregory Red, also known as Professor Gee

Wealth doesn't follow the individual; it follows the principles applied by the individual.

[This book is designed to deliver the message that the numbers couldn't.]

Copyright © 2025 by See Your Dollar, LLC
All rights reserved.
No part of this book may be reproduced, distributed, or transmitted in any form or by any means, including photocopying, recording, or other electronic or mechanical methods, without the prior written permission of the publisher, except in the case of brief quotations used for review purposes.

Disclaimer:
This book is for informational purposes only. The author and publisher assume no responsibility for errors or omissions.
Author: Gregory Red

ISBN: [979-8-9927874-0-5]
ISBN: [979-8-9927874-1-2]
Published by: See Your Dollar, LLC
Website: SeeYourDollar.com
email: grow@seeyourdollar.com

YOU'RE GRANTED NO MORE & NO LESS EACH DAY

The Amount of TIME in ONE DAY

Hours	1	2	3	4	5	6	7	8	9	10	11	12
Minutes	60	120	180	240	300	360	420	480	540	600	660	720
Seconds	3,600	7,200	10,800	14,400	18,000	21,600	25,200	28,800	32,400	36,000	39,600	43,200
Hours	13	14	15	16	17	18	19	20	21	22	23	24
Minutes	780	840	900	960	1,020	1,080	1,140	1,200	1,260	1,320	1,380	1,440
Seconds	46,800	50,400	54,000	57,600	61,200	64,800	68,400	72,000	75,600	79,200	82,800	86,400

HOW ARE YOU SPENDING YOUR TIME?
DOES BALANCE EXIST WITHIN YOUR DAY?
(DO YOU FEEL THERE'S A BALANCE BETWEEN PERSONAL AND CAREER GROWTH AND THE TIME YOU SPEND ON WHAT BRINGS JOY AND FULFILLMENT TO YOU OR OTHERS?)

NO NEED TO RUSH; WITH NO TIME TO WASTE

	10 years	10 years	10 years	10 years	10 years	10 years	10 years	10 years	10 years	10 years
1	•	•	•	•	•	•	•	•	•	•
2	•	18	•	•	•	•	•	•	81	•
3	•	Y	•	•	•	•	•	•	To	•
4	•	E	•	•	•	•	•	•	100	•
5	•	A	•	•	•	•	•	•	Years	•
6	•	R	•	•	•	•	•	•	Old	•
7	•	S	•	•	•	•	•	•		•
8	•	•	•	•	•	•	•	•	•	•
9	•	•	•	•	•	•	•	•	•	•
	•	•	•	•	•	•	•	•	•	•
	10	20	30	40	50	60	70	80	90	100

PATIENCE IS A VIRTUE

Content

Dedication
Introduction (pg. 1)
"A Few Words Before We Begin" (pg. 4)

PART 1: THE FOUNDATION OF GENERATIONAL WEALTH
Pt. 1 Chapter 1 - Generational Wealth (pg. 8)
Pt. 1 Chapter 2 - Remain Mentally Sharp (pg. 11)
Pt. 1 Chapter 3 - Timeless Qualities (pg. 18)
Pt. 1 Chapter 4 - Work Smarter; Not Harder (pg. 24)
Pt. 1 Chapter 5 - A Part of Understanding The Game (pg. 36)

PART 2: PROSPERITY
Pt. 2 Chapter 1 - Forever Growth Plus Progress (pg. 43)
Pt. 2 Chapter 2 - Respect The Game (pg. 56)

PART 3: BUILDING STRONG CHARACTER
The Importance of Parts 3 & 4 (pg. 61)
Pt. 3 Chapter 1 - Humility (pg. 63)
Pt. 3 Chapter 2 - Integrity (pg. 68)
Pt. 3 Chapter 3 - Discipline (pg. 77)
Pt. 3 Chapter 4 - Accountability (pg. 85)
Pt. 3 Chapter 5 - Gratitude (pg. 88)

PART 4: THE INGREDIENTS TO SUCCESS
Pt. 4 Chapter 1 - Mindset (pg. 92)
Pt. 4 Chapter 2 - Characteristics (pg. 136)
Pt. 4 Chapter 3 - The Foundation (pg. 145)
Pt. 4 Chapter 4 - The Value Chain (pg. 168)
Conclusion (pg. 182)
About The Author

FINANCIAL LITERACY AND BOUNDLESS & PERPETUAL LEARNING ENABLES OPTIMAL FREEDOM

YOUR WISDOM CAPACITY IS INFINITE/LIMITLESS

Dedicated

To

You

Dedication

This book is dedicated to those navigating the game of life, searching for clarity, guidance, and a foundation built on principles that foster true generational wealth. It is for those who understand that wealth is more than money. True wealth is the character, mindset, and values we pass down that determine our legacy.

To the parents and mentors already instilling wisdom in their children, may this book serve as an additional tool to reinforce the lessons of integrity, accountability, humility, discipline, dedication, perseverance, ambition, resilience, faith, and rational thinking.

To those who lack a mentor, guardian, or someone to serve as a guide—who must teach themselves the lessons that life did not readily provide—this book is FOR YOU. May it serve as a compass, pointing you toward the principles, traits, and habits that will equip you for success, no matter where you start.

And to the next generation, who will inherit not just the assets but the mindset necessary to sustain true prosperity—may these principles be your foundation. Because when we pass down the habits of discipline, foresight, strong communication skills, financial literacy, and a commitment to lifelong learning, we don't just build wealth—we build individuals who can withstand any storm and create their own path forward.

This is more than a book. It's a blueprint for those ready to take ownership of their future and ensure that the wheel of generational success never stops rolling.

Introduction

Introduction

I was born uptown in the 3rd Ward of New Orleans, Louisiana, and spent my early childhood living in various parts of the city. With family members spread across different neighborhoods—both within and outside of New Orleans—I had the opportunity to stay in their homes as if their house was my house. This experience exposed me to multiple urban communities, as well as one suburban community, at a young age. This early exposure to multiple neighborhoods not only helped me understand multiple perspectives and different ways of living, but it also laid the foundation for my ability to adapt to different environments throughout my life's journey.

My parents and I were victims of a systemic problem. My father was affected in a way that placed hardships on my mother, who became a single parent and had to dedicate most of her time to working, just so we could have a roof over our heads and food on the table. I graduated high school with the reading skills of a first grader. But after turning 22 and stepping away from the fast life, I purchased courses that helped me improve my reading and comprehension skills, teaching me how to break down syllables in words. That period marked the beginning of my self-taught quest for knowledge.

Growing up, I faced many challenges. By the age of 13, I had started smoking marijuana, and by 15, I was involved in criminal activities. Before turning 21, I was a two-time convicted felon. Between the ages of 15 and 22, I lived a fast and dangerous life, making and losing money, with my life on the line every day. I experienced what most people in that life don't survive. Through God's grace, I did.

At the age of 22, I realized that the value of my life was worth more than the risk I was taking for money within the life of crime.

Therefore, at the age of 23, I stepped away from the fast life and channeled my attention towards a legitimate means of survival. I entered the trucking business, starting with a dually truck moving cars, which eventually led to me purchasing my first 18-wheeler. This experience gave me deep insight into how America's industrial companies operate. The money I earned from trucking helped me invest in real estate, where I bought rental properties and built houses. Which later led to me becoming a licensed contractor.

  After getting into real estate, I wanted to learn about investing in the stock market. In the process of trying to complete a fundamental analysis of companies, I realized I needed a better understanding of financial structure and accounting. So, I took an accounting course, which helped me gain a stronger grip on managing my finances. It also played a key role in helping me understand how the stock market operates. With that knowledge, I started connecting the dots between the industrial industry, real estate and the stock market. I began to see the larger American economic system. The bigger picture of how the game of America works became clearer to me.

  Having turned my life around, I'm now focused on helping others find a better path. I believe that understanding your finances and how money works is key to succeeding in America. By teaching financial literacy, we can help each other navigate this world. Once we understand how finances work, it can improve not only our personal lives but also the lives of our neighbors.

  I truly believe that by teaching one person at a time about their finances and how to navigate this world with a better understanding of money, that individual becomes more equipped to improve their life. Once they start applying this knowledge, they can demonstrate better financial habits. Through their actions and conscious efforts, they can then teach their neighbors to do the same. This ripple effect can lead to a community collectively doing better. As more communities improve, this progress can expand to society, then to the nation, and eventually beyond. But it all starts with dedicating effort to teaching one person at a time.

"A Few Words Before We Begin"

Your
"POTENTIAL"
Is Defined By The Depth Of
THE KNOWLEDGE THAT YOU POSSESS!
Your
"GREATNESS"
Is Determined By <u>How Effectively You Apply</u>
THE KNOWLEDGE THAT YOU POSSESS!

If A Man Can Articulate An Extent Of Knowledge
But His Actions Is Free Of The Application Of That Knowledge,
HE IS MERELY A MAN OF WORDS; NOT DEEDS!
Even Though
He May "Sound Smart" And "Highly Intelligent",
HIS ACTIONS REVEAL A LACK OF TRUE WISDOM!

THEREFORE, <u>TRUE WEALTH</u> IS DEMONSTRATED THROUGH <u>YOUR ACTIONS</u>
AND <u>YOUR ACTIONS</u> REFLECT THE DEPTH OF <u>YOUR WISDOM</u>.
<u>AS YOUR WISDOM IS ROOTED</u>
IN THE KNOWLEDGE YOU "<u>ACQUIRE</u>" AND "<u>PUT INTO PRACTICE</u>"!

The Illusion of Wealth vs. the Reality of Life

In this life, there is no denying the importance of money. We need it to survive, to provide for our families, and to create comfort in our daily lives. The pursuit of financial stability is necessary, and money itself is a powerful tool—<u>but it is not *everything*</u>.

Too often, people believe that wealth is the answer to all of life's problems. They beleve that having more money will bring them happiness, fulfillment, and purpose. But the truth is, money can only do so much. It can buy experiences, but not *genuine connection*. It can open doors, but it cannot walk the path for you. It can provide security, but it cannot guarantee peace of mind.

Before we chase after money as if it's the ultimate prize, we must understand what it *cannot* give us. Because if we don't, we risk losing the things that truly matter—our relationships, our peace of mind, our time, and our sense of purpose—all while chasing something that was never meant to replace those things.

Money was never meant to replace those things. It was only meant to serve as a tool to help us navigate life and support us in the pursuit of what truly matters. <u>It can provide opportunities, open doors, and create access. But it cannot give meaning, fulfillment, or lasting happiness on its own. When we understand this, we stop chasing wealth as if it's the destination and start using it as the tool it was always meant to be.</u>

Money Is Only A Tool:

Here are just a few things that money will never be able to buy:

1. <u>*Peace of Mind*</u> – Money can give you temporary relief from stress, but true peace comes from within. It comes from knowing you've done right by yourself and others.

2. <u>*True Friendship*</u> – Money can attract people to you. But it can't create genuine, unconditional friendships built on trust, loyalty, and

mutual respect.

3. _Self-Worth_ – Money can make you feel important in the eyes of the world. But true self-worth comes from knowing who you are beyond material possessions.

4. _Wisdom_ – You can pay for education. But wisdom comes from experience, self-reflection, and learning from life's lessons.

5. _Health_ – Money can help you afford healthcare. But it cannot guarantee good health, nor can it buy back time lost due to neglecting your well-being.

6. _Time_ – Money can make life easier. But it cannot turn back the clock, undo regrets, or give you more time with those who have passed.

7. _Respect_ – People might admire your wealth. But real respect is earned through your actions, character, and how you treat others.

8. _Happiness_ – Money can buy entertainment, distractions, and temporary pleasure, but true happiness comes from purpose, fulfillment, and meaningful relationships.

9. _A Good Reputation_ – Money can buy publicity. But a solid reputation is built through integrity, honesty, and consistency over time.

10. _Purpose_ – You can be rich and still feel lost. Purpose comes from understanding your role in the world and pursuing something bigger than just wealth.

11. _A Loving Family_ – Money can provide for your family's needs. But it cannot build strong relationships, trust, or the love shared through quality time and genuine connection.

12. _Spiritual Fulfillment_ – No amount of money can fill the void that comes from lacking a deeper sense of meaning, faith, or connection to something greater than yourself.

PART 1: THE FOUNDATION OF GENERATIONAL WEALTH

Pt. 1 Chapter 1 Generational Wealth

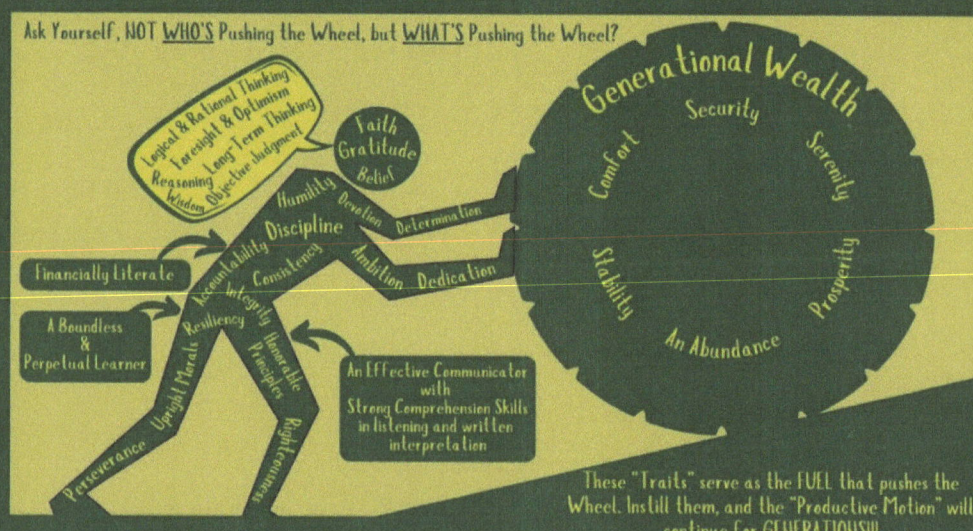

INTANGIBLE WEALTH

Imagine a wheel rolling forward, driven by your effort. At first, you see yourself pushing the wheel—step by step, stride by stride— with dedication, determination, and focus. But pause for a moment. Step back and ask yourself: What is it within you that's allowing you to push this wheel forward in the first place?

It's not just your hands on the wheel—it's your character that drives it. Your discipline! Your resilience! Your ambition! Your integrity! The ability to stay accountable and keep moving forward, even when the road is rough. These aren't just traits. They're the fuel behind the momentum.

Now, step back even further. Let's remove you from the picture. Instead of seeing yourself, imagine those very characteristics—dedication, consistency, discipline—acting like invisible forces, pushing that wheel forward on their own.

Here's the key: If we instill these characteristics in our children, they won't need us physically behind them, constantly doing the pushing. Therefore, without our presence, the wheel will keep moving due to the values we've left behind. If we embed discipline, accountability, and resilience in them, the momentum will forever continue, just like a wheel with its own motion.

And if they pass those traits on to their children, the cycle won't break. The wheel will keep rolling, generation after generation, driven not by external force, but by the values and principles rooted deep within them.

This is how we build generational progress. When we focus not only on pushing the wheel ourselves but also on ensuring that the next generation understands <u>how to push the wheel for themselves</u>— through their mindset, character, and habits—then we've done something truly lasting. The wheel will always roll, long after we're gone, because the essence of what drives it will be instilled and will never disappear.

And that's how legacies are built—through character, not just through wealth or guidance, but by passing down the very tools of perseverance.

Therefore, if we truly seek Generational Wealth, we cannot depend solely on our presence, nor can we rely on the material possessions—money, assets, and estates—that we leave behind. Wealth, in its truest form, is not just what we pass down in our hands but what we embed in the hearts and minds of our children.

If we want the legacy to last, we must instill Generational Principles—honor, discipline, integrity, and resilience—because it is these principles that will sustain the forward motion for ages, long after we are gone. This is what will secure the prosperity and well-being of our children's children, their children, and every generation that follows.

Therefore, the money, businesses, and assets we leave behind will serve only as tools. They will be helpful, but secondary. The true foundation of wealth will always be in the mindset, the character, and the unshakable principles we engrain within them. Because with those, no matter what they face, they will always have the ability to build, sustain, and pass the legacy forward.

[This is the recipe to true Generation Wealth]

Pt. 1 Chapter 2 Remain Mentally Sharp

Intelligence combined with Determination PAVES THE WAY to Great Success, while Ignorance Paired with Action Leads to Stagnation or, even worse, RUIN.

Knowledge is Truly Power. But the True Value lies in how you APPLY IT,

NEVER STOP FEEDING YOUR BRAIN

The most influential men and women in history were those who expanded their knowledge beyond the confines of traditional schooling. They studied what was needed to earn their diplomas, certificates, or degrees, but didn't stop there. **They took the initiative to educate themselves beyond the school curriculum and outside the classroom through Reading Books, Learning from Gurus, Seeking Mentors, and Gaining Real-World Experience.**

School gives most people a foundation, but the ones who truly make an <u>**impact are the ones who never stop learning** on their own.</u>

The most successful people made learning a lifelong habit, understanding that real success comes from **gaining knowledge that sets them apart in the real world.** Those who continued to expand their knowledge found themselves Ahead of the Curve and a Step Ahead in Life's Challenges. As a result of their dedication to learning, they gained a competitive advantage that <u>**fueled their AMBITIONS**</u> and <u>**SHARPENED their MINDS, giving them the upper hand in the GAME of LIFE**</u>.

To be great, you must be Knowledgeable! That's why you should read everything you can that provides valuable knowledge. The more you expose yourself to different ideas, perspectives, and information, the better equipped you'll be to handle life's opportunities and challenges. Suppose you're more comfortable familiarizing yourself with a subject through YouTube or any other digital platform. In that case, you should use the Digital Platform as a tool to feed your brain, educate yourself, expand your knowledge, acquire meaningful knowledge, enhance your worldly intelligence, and broaden your perspective. You should follow that same procedure if you're more comfortable with audiobooks.

Food for thought: If you're ever struggling with finding in-depth knowledge on a subject or topic that you're interested in, 9 times out of 10, someone has already written about the subject or topic. And the Knowledge is sheltered within the pages of a book, article, or document. Therefore, your only job is to find and read the information (most of the time, it's in a book). **In today's time, with the development of advanced digital technology that leverages artificial intelligence, YOU HAVE THE WORLD'S GREATEST "SEARCH ENGINE" AT YOUR FINGERTIPS. WHICH IS ACCESSIBLE THROUGH DEVICES LIKE SMARTPHONES, TABLETS, LAPTOPS AND COMPUTERS, [MAKING LIMITLESS KNOWLEDGE AND INFORMATION JUST A FEW CLICKS AWAY & IN THE PALM OF YOUR HAND.]** Therefore, if you search for the Knowledge of your interest, you'll find a platter of books, sources, articles, and more filled with an abundance of readable Knowledge.

So with all due respect, "IT'S YOUR JOB TO SEEK THE KNOWLEDGE!" NO ONE ELSE IS TO BLAME FOR THE KNOWLEDGE THAT YOU DO NOT SEEK! You're in control of you!

You are responsible for what you have learned and everything you haven't learned yet that's waiting to be discovered by you!

Gaining wisdom from others is one of the smartest and most efficient ways to grow. Think about it like this: no one lives long enough to learn everything independently. Life's timeline is vast, and the experiences, lessons, and knowledge from generations before us are too valuable to ignore. That's why it's essential to study and learn from the journeys of others. The books we read should include biographies and autobiographies of men and women who have achieved greatness in their unique paths—whether it be their Mission, Career, Profession, Trade, Calling, or Contribution to The World. By learning from their successes and failures, we gain insight that can guide our own journey.

There's SO MUCH Great Value in learning from the knowledge and experience of others [especially from the MISTAKES of others - IT CAN SAVE YOU SO MUCH TIME BY BEING AN OBSERVANT & HEEDFUL STUDENT OF LIFE]. It's a sign of wisdom to seek insight from those around you [insight from those that's Younger, Older, Successful and Unsuccessful]. For instance, you can learn from the Unsuccessful by understanding their MISSTEPS & MISTAKES. Which in return grants you the opportunity to AVOID SIMILAR PITFALLS & MISTAKES!

   Momentarily, I would like to build on Marcus Garvey's perspective. He suggested that you read, learn, and study history relentlessly until you master it. **It will help you connect the dots and give a degree of clarity to how civilization became what it is that you currently know it as. It can help you understand YOURSELF, YOUR ORIGIN, and the FORCES THAT SHAPED WHO YOU ARE as of TODAY.** This means you should dive into your own national history, explore the history of the world, and understand social and industrial history. Study the evolution of different sciences and their impact on society. Above all, we should focus on the **History of Humanity**—**the journey of mankind through time**. Understanding how people lived, adapted, and overcame challenges will give you a broader perspective on life and a deeper understanding of human nature, which is invaluable in navigating your own path. **YOU SHOULD KNOW THE HISTORY OF YOUR RACE & ETHNICITY and THE HISTORY OF OTHER RACES & ETHNICITIES**. ****When studying history, prepare yourself for the possibility of encountering information that may be disturbing, unsettling, provocative, or even anger you. However, remember and keep in mind that the goal and purpose of studying history IS NOT to Fuel Anger or Dwell in Anger, but to Gain an Understanding of how life has evolved into what it is today while Fostering a Deeper Understanding of the Journey that SHAPED THE PRESENT!*

  If you don't understand what happened before your time or what is currently unfolding around you, you will struggle to grasp the world you live in fully, the role you play, and the "game" you're navigating. **[It's helpful to understand the past events of the world and the events shaping it right now within the present.]** Without this understanding, you risk living ignorant of the world and humanity's progress. The key to making the most out of life lies in knowing how

the world works and why it works that way. To gain that knowledge, you must lean on the wisdom and experiences of those who came before you, studying the records they've left behind to guide you forward.

Think about this: By reading good books and studying material that was written or left behind by a great man or woman, you allow yourself the opportunity to get acquainted with the MIND of that great person. This is a valuable experience because if the person is dead and gone, you will never come in social contact with that person. But through their books and other documents, you will forever have the opportunity to explore their thoughts, ideas, beliefs, perspectives, and opinions. Therefore, you will forever have a piece of their mindset without ever meeting them in real-life.

Always push yourself toward the things you want to achieve, and never stop or give up until you reach your goal. If others have accomplished similar objectives, then so can you. Their success is living proof that it's possible. The journey may be challenging, but persistence, dedication, and education will always bring you closer to your desires.

However, sometimes the only thing holding us back is the lack of knowledge of how to achieve what we're striving for. **This is why knowledge is power.** The more you learn and apply, the better equipped you are to navigate obstacles and turn your goals into reality.

No one is ever too old to learn, and growth has no age limit. Take full advantage of the knowledge and resources available to you, whether through books, mentors, experiences, or new opportunities. Every day is a chance to learn something new, and the more you seek out knowledge, the more you'll continue to evolve and improve throughout your life.

You can learn about any topic imaginable by simply reading about it. You just have to search for the information.

The world is full of knowledge, waiting for you to discover it. Mostly, everything that you want to know about is out there. Therefore, you just have to seek it with determination. Never stop searching, questioning, and exploring until you find the answers you're looking for. **The more knowledge you gain, the more tools you'll have to shape your future and achieve your goals.**

Master the skill of seeking the knowledge when you need the knowledge. **Because what truly matters is having the ability to search for and access the information you need when you need it. If you master the skill of seeking knowledge, you'll always be equipped to find the right answers, solve problems, and adapt to any situation life throws your way.**

In Closing, always remember this: Refer to your **BRAIN** as if it were a software that can be programmed and upgraded. The more you learn, the more valuable data you download into your system. By becoming a lifelong & habitual learner, you can remain up-to-date, just like any software that constantly receives updates to improve its performance. But here's the key—just as software can be intentionally programmed, <u>**"SO CAN YOU" be intentionally programmed**</u>. When you control what you learn and focus on the knowledge you truly want, you're reprogramming yourself. Instead of being limited by the way the school system and your surroundings (society, community, and upbringing) may have initially shaped your thinking, you gain the power to rewrite your own mental code, like adding new features, advantages, and tools to help you navigate the Game of Life on your terms. Remember, <u>**YOU'RE IN CONTROL OF YOUR MENTAL PROGRAMMING!!!**</u>

[Don't Play Yourself]

[Always have up-to-date knowledge]

[Develop and maintain a Keen Eye for Detail]

& [Be as attentive with your vision as you are with your hearing]… in other words, Listen Closely With Your "EYES" just as well as You Do with your "EARS" - letting your "EYES" hear the details too!

[Appreciate the Journey!]

[And remember, "The Struggle Is Ordained"] So KEEP PUSHING & TRUST THE PROCESS

Real Wealth Is Knowledge!

Pt. 1 Chapter 3 Timeless Qualities

TIMELESS QUALITIES: (AND SOME CORE INGREDIENTS OF A PROSPEROUS PERSON)

COMMUNICATION
- Spoken Communication
- Written Communication
- "Skilled in both expression and understanding"
- "An effective communicator with strong comprehension skills in listening and/or interpretation"
- The understanding of grammar structure, vocabulary, and how to use a dictionary plays a critical role in enhancing someone's ability to interpret and comprehend written communication.

A HABITUAL LEARNER
- Continuous Growth
- A habitual learner is not confined to formal education—they find opportunities to learn in everyday life, whether through conversations, experiences, or even failures, making learning an ongoing journey.
- By developing these skills, readers not only interpret text more effectively but also gain the ability to engage with increasingly complex material, enriching their overall literacy and critical thinking abilities.

FINANCIAL LITERACY
- PREVENTS BAD DEBT
- PROMOTES INDEPENDENCE
- BUILDS WEALTH
- REDUCES STRESS

IMPROVED READING FLUENCY   BETTER CRITICAL THINKING   INCREASED CONFIDENCE

Spoken communication

Spoken communication refers to the process of conveying information, ideas, thoughts, or emotions through verbal expression. It involves using spoken language, including words, tone, pitch, and rhythm, to interact with others. This form of communication often relies on face-to-face interactions, phone calls, or any medium where speech is used to exchange messages. Spoken communication is typically accompanied by non-verbal indications such as gestures, facial expressions, and body language, which help enhance the understanding and emotional context of the message.

Written communication

Written communication refers to the process of expressing information, ideas, or thoughts through written symbols, such as letters, words, and punctuation. It includes any form of communication where the message is conveyed in a readable format, such as letters, emails, text messages, reports, books, or social media posts.

Grammar Structure, Vocabulary, and How to Use a Dictionary:

Grammar Structure:

Grammar Structure Improves Sentence Understanding - Grammar provides the rules for constructing and interpreting sentences. Knowing grammar helps readers understand how words are organized and how ideas are connected.

It Clarifies Meaning - Understanding syntax (sentence structure) enables a reader to distinguish between literal and implied meanings, which reduces confusion.

It Interprets Tone and Nuance - Grammar affects tone, tense, and emphasis, all of which contribute to deeper comprehension.

- Grammar is Important in Understanding Others: When you know grammar rules, it's easier to interpret what others say or write.

Think of grammar as the rules of a game—once you learn them, you can "play" with language more confidently and effectively!

Vocabulary:

Vocabulary Expands Understanding - A broad vocabulary allows readers to understand a wide range of words, expressions, and ideas without constantly needing external references.

It Interprets Context - Strong vocabulary skills help in inferring/gathering meanings of unfamiliar words from context, <u>which enhances fluid reading</u>.

It Builds Precision - Knowing subtle differences between synonyms allows for a better grasp of the exact meaning a writer intends to convey.

Using a Dictionary:

Using a Dictionary Clarifies Unknown Words - A dictionary is a powerful tool for resolving ambiguities/vagueness in meaning, pronunciation, and usage.

It Improves Word Retention - Regular dictionary use helps reinforce vocabulary knowledge, making it easier to recognize and recall words later.

It Encourages Independent Learning - The ability to look up unfamiliar words fosters self-reliance and curiosity, <u>which can deepen one's comprehension over time.</u>

How The Improvement of These Three Qualities Enhances Comprehension Skills:

They Improve The Fluency of Reading - Mastering grammar and vocabulary enables smoother reading, reducing the effort spent on decoding individual sentences and words.

They Enhance Better Critical Thinking - With a solid grammar and word meaning foundation, readers can focus on analyzing and interpreting a text's broader themes and arguments.

They Increase Confidence - When readers understand the rules and tools of language, they approach written communication with greater confidence, *which leads to more effective comprehension.*

Habitual Learner

A habitual learner is someone who consistently seeks to acquire knowledge, develop skills, and expand their understanding as part of their daily routine. Learning is not just an occasional activity for them—it is a way of life. They are driven by curiosity, discipline, and a growth mindset, always looking for opportunities to explore new ideas, solve problems, or improve themselves.

Key Traits of a Habitual Learner

1. Curiosity - They are naturally inquisitive and ask questions about the world around them.

2. Consistency - Learning becomes integral to their daily habits, such as reading, researching, practicing, or reflecting.

3. Adaptability - They embrace change and seek new knowledge to adapt to evolving circumstances.

4. Self-Motivation - They learn for personal growth, not just for external rewards or recognition.

5. *Resourcefulness - They know how to find and use resources—books, online courses, mentors, or experiences—to support their learning.*

6. Reflection - They regularly analyze their experiences and apply lessons learned to future situations.

These are Some Benefits of Being a Habitual Learner

1. Continuous Growth - They always improve, gain new skills, and stay relevant in their personal and professional lives.

2. Resilience - Their willingness to learn helps them overcome challenges and adapt to setbacks.

3. Fulfillment - The joy of discovery and personal development brings a sense of accomplishment and purpose.

4. Broad Perspective - *By exploring diverse topics, they develop a deeper and more nuanced understanding of the world.*

Financial Literacy

Financial literacy is understanding and effectively using financial knowledge and skills to manage money and make informed decisions about personal finances. *It involves knowing how money works, including earning, saving, spending, investing, and borrowing.*

Key Components of Financial Literacy

1. Budgeting - Knowing how to plan and track income and expenses to ensure you live within your means.

2. Saving and Investing - Understanding the importance of saving for emergencies and future goals and how to grow money through investments like stocks, bonds, mutual funds, etc.

3. Debt Management - Learning how to borrow money responsibly, understand interest rates, and avoid getting into excessive debt.

4. Understanding Credit - Knowing how credit scores work and how to use credit cards or loans wisely without harming your financial health.

5. Taxes - Being aware of how taxes work, including income taxes and deductions, to manage finances effectively.

6. Planning for the Future - Setting financial goals, building retirement plans, and understanding insurance to protect yourself from unexpected events.

Why Is Financial Literacy Important?

It Helps Prevent Debt - It helps you avoid financial mistakes like overspending or taking on too much debt.

It Helps Build Wealth - With financial literacy, you can grow your money through smart saving and investing.

It Helps Promote Independence - It empowers you to make financial decisions without relying on others.

It Helps Reduce Stress - Managing money well gives you peace of mind and financial security.

<u>*In simple terms, financial literacy gives you the tools to take control of your money so you can achieve your goals and secure your future.*</u>

Pt. 1 Chapter 4
Work Smarter; Not Harder

**WORK SMARTER, NOT HARDER
&
PLAY THE GAME-OF-LIFE WITH THE DEVELOPED SKILL OF "ACTIVE LISTENING" WHILE LEVERAGING "TTS" TECHNOLOGY**

What is Active Listening

Active listening is the skill of fully focusing on, understanding, and engaging with what someone else is saying. It goes beyond simply hearing words—it involves giving your full attention to the speaker and processing their message.

A key component of active listening is <u>"PAYING ATTENTION</u>." Which focuses solely on the process of eliminating distractions and focusing entirely on the speaker [while not just hearing words, but understanding the tone, intent, and emotions behind what's being said].

It is important for Us as a People to develop the skill of "Active Listening." Below are a few reasons why!

1. Active listening fosters trust and understanding. When someone feels genuinely heard, they're more likely to open up, which strengthens personal and professional relationships.

2. Miscommunication often happens when we don't listen carefully. By actively listening, we ensure we understand the intended message, reducing misunderstandings and conflicts.

3. When we truly listen to someone, we gain insight into their perspective, feelings, and experiences. This helps us connect on a deeper level and reduces bias or judgment.

4. Active listening helps de-escalate conflicts by showing the other person that their concerns are heard and valued. This creates a space for collaborative problem-solving.

- For example, repeating the other person's point ("I understand that you're upset because...") can diffuse tension during an argument. *It really helps when the next person feels as if they were truly heard.*

5. Listening actively allows us to absorb and retain more information in school, work, or personal conversations. It's a foundational skill for personal development.

- Example: A student who listens carefully in class is more likely to succeed than one who passively hears the lesson.

6. **It Builds Community and Collaboration** - <u>As a society, active listening helps bridge separation [amongst the POLARIZED, FRAGMENTED, DIVIDED, AND DISUNITED]. It's a key skill for leaders, negotiators, and anyone involved in teamwork. It ensures that all voices are heard and valued, creating more inclusive and productive environments.</u>

- <u>Example: In a community meeting, actively listening to different viewpoints can lead to solutions that benefit everyone.</u>

7. Active listening helps us recognize and respond to emotions in ourselves and others. This makes us better at managing relationships and handling interpersonal challenges.

ACTIVE LISTENING IS NOT JUST A SKILL—IT'S A CORNERSTONE OF EFFECTIVE COMMUNICATION AND MEANINGFUL CONNECTION. IN A WORLD WHERE DISTRACTIONS ARE EVERYWHERE AND PEOPLE OFTEN FEEL UNHEARD, DEVELOPING THIS SKILL HELPS US BECOME MORE COMPASSIONATE, UNDERSTANDING, AND IMPACTFUL IN OUR INTERACTIONS.

WHEN WE, AS A PEOPLE, ACTIVELY LISTEN, WE FOSTER STRONGER BONDS, RESOLVE CONFLICTS, AND BUILD A CULTURE OF RESPECT AND EMPATHY—QUALITIES THAT ARE ESSENTIAL FOR THRIVING IN ANY COMMUNITY OR SOCIETY.

What is "TTS" Technology (Text-To-Speech Technology)

Text-To-Speech (TTS) is technology that converts written text into spoken words using synthetic or natural-sounding voices. It is widely used in accessibility tools, virtual assistants, audiobooks, and more.

TTS technology shifts the burden from manual effort to automated assistance, allowing you to focus on understanding and applying information rather than spending unnecessary energy on the act of reading. It embodies the saying "<u>WORK SMARTER; NOT HARDER</u>"! It offers several benefits, especially when it comes to multitasking and accessibility.

Below are a few Benefits of TTS Technology:

1) It helps individuals with visual impairments, dyslexia, and physical disabilities in relation to handling printed material, or individuals with other reading challenges in connection to the NON-FLUENT Reader. It also helps the FLUENT Reader.

2) It allows users to listen to text-based content like E-Books, Articles, Emails and anything you can get in a PDF Documents while performing other tasks, such as driving, exercising, cooking, doing laundry, cleaning and etc.

3) It helps save time by allowing you to "read" while your hands and eyes are occupied.

4) Listening and reading simultaneously can improve your comprehension and memory qualities. Which is beneficial for auditory learners who absorb information better when they hear it.

5) It assists in pronunciation and comprehension when you're learning a new language by hearing how words and sentences are spoken.

6) It helps speed up the consumption of lengthy documents, reports, and Multiple Books! This allows you to convert time spent

commuting or doing chores into productive learning or work time.

Think about it like this: "TTS Technology is like being part of a group reading session where others take turns reading, and your role is to listen and comprehend the material. The most important aspect, whether you're the one reading or not, is understanding what's being said. With TTS, the technology takes over the reading, allowing you to focus entirely on processing and absorbing the information. Just as in a group, comprehension is key, and listening actively ensures you're fully engaged with the content." ***<u>This analogy emphasizes how TTS supports comprehension, even when you're not actively "reading" yourself, by allowing you to focus on the meaning rather than the act of reading</u>. Understanding grammar structure becomes the backbone of this process, allowing you to mentally organize and interpret what you hear, maintain focus on meaning, and fully engage with the content. Without a strong grasp of grammar, the text might sound like a stream of unrelated words, making comprehension difficult.

Active Listening Meets "TTS": Your Ultimate Digital Assistant:

Imagine you're sitting with someone really wise—like a grandparent, a teacher, or even a coach who has a deep understanding of life. When they talk, they share things that make you think, open your mind, and maybe even teach you something you didn't know. Now, the cool thing is, you don't have to do much. You don't have to dig through books or go out and experience their years of life—they've already done that for you. Within those moments, your job is simple; you only have to <u>"listen and learn."</u>

That's what TTS technology is like. It's like sitting down with that wise person, except instead of a human, it's the technology delivering the information. When TTS reads a book, article, or even a text message to you, it's basically saying, "Hey, let me do the hard work of reading this text. You just sit back, focus, and listen." It's taking knowledge from a page and putting it directly in your ears.

It's like having a mentor who follows you around, always ready to explain something or tell you a story. You don't have to stop your life to gain wisdom or knowledge. It works around your schedule and fits within your agenda. And it operates on demand at your request.

<u>The more you know, the better decisions you can make. Knowledge is like a superpower—it helps you think bigger, dream bigger, and do better. TTS gives you a shortcut to that power. Instead of sitting down with a book or a wise person and spending hours learning, you can absorb the same knowledge just by listening. It saves you time, makes learning more accessible, and gives you the freedom to keep living your life while still leveling up your understanding.</u>

So, in a way, TTS technology is like having a personal mentor, guide, or wise person who's always there to share what they know. [The beautiful part is, YOU'RE IN CONTROL OF THE TECHNOLOGY. THEREFORE, YOU GIVE THE TECHNOLOGY THE INFORMATION & SUBJECTS THAT YOU WANT TO KNOW MORE ABOUT. YOU SELECT THE BOOKS, ARTICLES, AND DOCUMENTS THAT YOU WANT THE TECHNOLOGY TO READ TO YOU]. The only difference is, instead of a person, it's a voice powered by technology, and it's ready to help you grow wherever you are. All you have to do is listen.

It's like if that wise person came to you and said, "Don't worry about finding time to read all this stuff—I've got it. Just listen, and I'll explain everything while you go about your day."

It's like sitting down with a wise person because, in both scenarios, the focus is on "Active Listening."

When you sit down with a wise person, the expectation is that you listen carefully, reflect on their words, and grasp the meaning behind what they're saying. Similarly, with TTS technology, you rely on your listening skills to absorb and understand the content being read aloud. In both cases:

- The focus is not on doing the talking (or reading) but on interpreting and comprehending what is being shared.
- Your role is to engage mentally with the message, making connections and applying what you hear.

Just as you wouldn't interrupt a wise person mid-sentence to respeak their words, TTS encourages you to let the content flow naturally, training your ability to keep up with ideas as they unfold.

Whether you're listening to a wise person or TTS, the key to understanding lies in Active Listening—paying attention to tone, context, and structure.

Sitting with a wise person grants you access to their wisdom and knowledge, potentially changing your perspective or teaching you something new. TTS technology <u>democratizes</u> this concept, allowing you to access books, articles, or even complex ideas that might have otherwise been out of reach due to time constraints or reading challenges. The medium changes (person vs. technology), but the result is the same: learning and growth through listening.

Just as a wise person speaks to you so you don't have to read their ideas in a book, TTS eliminates the need for you to manually read text, freeing you to focus on understanding the message while multitasking or relaxing. The common factor here is efficiency: wisdom or knowledge is delivered directly, bypassing unnecessary steps.

All you need to do is listen. Whether the voice is that of a wise mentor or TTS, the primary skill required is your ability to pay attention and comprehend the material being shared. This emphasizes that your capacity for learning and understanding doesn't depend on whether you're actively reading or passively listening—what matters is your willingness to focus and absorb the message.

Listening is a Gateway to Knowledge

Sitting with a wise person and using TTS both center on the art of listening, a skill that unlocks the potential for growth, understanding, and enlightenment. The difference is only in the source: one is human, and the other is technological. However, the essence is the same—<u>when you truly listen, you open yourself up to new ideas, insights, and opportunities to learn, whether from a mentor's words or the voice of a TTS reader.</u>

If You're Not Leveraging Audiobooks and Text-To-Speech Technology, You're Missing Out On An Easy Way to Boost Your Mental Growth:

Most people fail to acknowledge how little time they have for manual reading. And because of that, they miss out on the opportunity to use TTS technology, which can fit seamlessly into their busy lives. They're missing the benefits of utilizing TTS technology, which allows them to listen to content while commuting, cooking, exercising, or even relaxing, turning those small moments into opportunities to learn and grow. Without it, valuable information and knowledge often remain out of reach.

People who insist on solely sitting down and manually reading books, articles, and documents might be missing out on some major advantages that TTS technology offers. While there's nothing wrong with enjoying traditional reading, sticking to it exclusively can limit how much knowledge and information you can absorb in your busy life.

Many people fail to realize that their busy day-to-day schedules leave them with little to no time to sit down and manually read. Below are a few reasons why:

1. People juggle work, school, family, and personal obligations. These constant demands often take priority over sitting down with a book, article, or document, leaving reading as something

they *intend* to do but rarely get around to. In a typical day, people prioritize tasks like commuting, cooking, cleaning, or caring for others over finding quiet time to read. Even when they get a free moment, they may prefer relaxing or unwinding instead of focusing on dense text. Many people already spend hours on screens for work or social media, so the idea of sitting down to read manually feels exhausting or like an added chore. People assume they'll find time later in the day to read, but that time rarely comes because they underestimate how packed their schedules are.
2. When you manually read, you have to dedicate time and focus solely on the act of reading. This means sitting down, opening the book or article, and making sure you're fully immersed. If your schedule is tight, this limits how much you can actually get through in a day.
3. For many, reading speed is slower than listening speed, especially with dense or complex material. People often stop, reread, or take breaks, which slows down the process. With TTS, you can adjust the playback speed to match your ability to process information, which means you can often listen to content faster than you can read it. This makes it possible to consume significantly more information in the same amount of time.
4. Not everyone has the time, energy, or physical ability to sit and read. Eye strain, fatigue, or even learning disabilities like dyslexia can make reading challenging for some. With TTS, People can bypass these challenges entirely. TTS makes content accessible to everyone, regardless of their ability to read manually. By ignoring TTS, people miss the chance to effortlessly engage with material they might otherwise struggle with if they manually read it themselves.
5. Sometimes, the idea of sitting down and reading a dense book or article can feel overwhelming. People often procrastinate because it feels like a big commitment. With TTS, you don't have to face that hurdle. TTS removes the mental block of "sitting down to read" and allows you to jump into the material effortlessly.

People who avoid TTS might be holding themselves back from starting or finishing something because they're stuck in the mindset that sitting down and manually reading is the only way to absorb readable information truly.
6. Reading requires undivided attention. If you're manually reading, you can't do much else at the same time. With TTS, you can multitask while learning. For example, you can listen to an audiobook while driving to work or read an article while doing laundry. People who refuse to use TTS are missing out on the ability to make the most of their time by combining TTS with whatever task they're juggling at that time.
7. Some people struggle with retention when reading because they're more auditory learners—they remember things better when they hear them. With TTS, listening activates a different part of your brain, which can help some people better understand and retain information. By avoiding TTS, auditory learners might miss out on a learning method that works better for them.
8. If you rely only on manual reading, your learning is confined to when you can sit down with a book or device. This limits how much new information you can access. With TTS, you can listen to books, articles, and documents anywhere—while traveling, exercising, or even relaxing with your eyes closed. This opens up far more opportunities to engage with new material throughout your day. By not using TTS, people are essentially turning down the chance to learn more often than they think.
9. Sitting for long periods while reading can be physically tiring, and staring at screens or printed text for too long can lead to eye strain or fatigue. With TTS, you can give your eyes and body a break by listening instead of reading. People who stick to manual reading exclusively might be unnecessarily straining themselves when they could give their minds and bodies some relief with TTS.

WHEN PEOPLE INSIST ON ONLY MANUALLY READING, THEY LIMIT HOW MUCH THEY CAN LEARN AND HOW EFFICIENTLY THEY CAN ABSORB INFORMATION.

TTS TECHNOLOGY DOESN'T HAVE TO REPLACE TRADITIONAL READING—IT CAN COMPLEMENT IT. BY INTEGRATING TTS INTO THEIR ROUTINES, PEOPLE CAN UNLOCK MORE OPPORTUNITIES TO ENGAGE WITH MATERIAL AND MAKE THEIR LEARNING PROCESS FASTER, EASIER, AND MORE EFFECTIVE. ****<u>BY REFUSING TO EMBRACE TTS, PEOPLE ARE ESSENTIALLY LEAVING KNOWLEDGE ON THE TABLE. THEY MISS THE CHANCE TO LEARN MORE, SAVE TIME, AND MAKE THEIR LIVES EASIER. THE FUTURE IS ABOUT WORKING SMARTER, NOT HARDER, AND TTS IS ONE OF THOSE TOOLS THAT HELPS BRIDGE THE GAP BETWEEN TIME, EFFORT, AND LEARNING.</u>

Identify & Address the ROOT of the Problem:

Some people struggle to use text-to-speech (TTS) technology effectively <u>because their REAL CHALLENGE lies in the ability to Actively Listen</u>—a skill that goes beyond simply hearing words. This issue highlights a deeper problem: <u>*if someone has trouble actively listening to TTS, it often reflects a broader difficulty in paying attention to and comprehending spoken information*</u>, whether it comes from technology or a real person in conversation.

Active Listening is the process of fully focusing on, understanding, and engaging with what is being said. It's not just about hearing words—it's about making sense of them, retaining the information, and responding appropriately. Whether you're listening to TTS or talking to a person, Active Listening ensures effective communication and comprehension.

If someone struggles to stay engaged with TTS, it's likely they also find it hard to stay focused during conversations with others.

Example: A person may zone out while TTS reads an article, just as they might lose focus when a friend explains something important.

Active Listening requires patience, which some people lack. They might interrupt TTS by pausing or skipping forward, just as they might cut off a person in conversation because they're unwilling to let the speaker finish.

The inability to actively listen doesn't just hinder someone's ability to use TTS—it affects their communication and relationships in daily life:

1. Conversations: They might frequently misunderstand others, miss important details, or zone out, causing frustration in their interactions.
2. Learning: In school or work settings, they might struggle to follow verbal instructions, lectures, or presentations.
3. Relationships: Poor listening skills can lead to conflicts, as they might appear inattentive, dismissive, or uninterested in what others are saying.

IF SOMEONE STRUGGLES WITH TTS BECAUSE THEY CAN'T ACTIVELY LISTEN, IT'S NOT JUST A TECH PROBLEM—IT'S A LIFE PROBLEM. THE SAME CHALLENGES THEY FACE WITH TTS LIKELY SPILL OVER INTO THEIR INTERACTIONS WITH PEOPLE, AFFECTING THEIR ABILITY TO CONNECT, LEARN, AND COMMUNICATE EFFECTIVELY. BUT STRENGTHENING ACTIVE LISTENING SKILLS WILL NOT ONLY MAKE TTS MORE USEFUL, BUT IT WILL ALSO IMPROVE HOW THEY NAVIGATE CONVERSATIONS, RELATIONSHIPS, AND OPPORTUNITIES IN EVERYDAY LIFE.

[ACTIVE LISTENING IS A CORE SKILL THAT SHOULD BE DEVELOPED, MAINTAINED, AND CONSTANTLY EXERCISED]

Pt. 1 Chapter 5
A Part of Understanding The Game

To Enhance Your Understanding of The GAME that you're in; You must Understand Economic Activity and Economic Data

Economic Activity

Economic activity refers to all the actions people, businesses, and governments take to produce, distribute, and consume goods and services in an economy. It is essentially the work and trade that happens to meet people's needs and wants.

Examples of Economic Activity

1. Production - Making goods or providing services, like a factory producing cars or a chef preparing food.

2. Distribution - Moving goods and services from producers to consumers, like shipping products or selling items in a store.

3. Consumption - Buying and using goods and services, like purchasing groceries or hiring a plumber.

Types of Economic Activities

1. Primary Activities - Directly using natural resources, like farming, fishing, or mining.

2. Secondary Activities - Transforming raw materials into finished goods, like manufacturing or construction.

3. Tertiary Activities - Providing services like healthcare, education, or retail.

4. Quaternary Activities - Knowledge-based services, like research, information technology, or financial planning.

Why Is Economic Activity Important?

It Drives Growth - Economic activity generates income for individuals, businesses, and governments, helping economies grow.

It Creates Jobs - It provides employment opportunities for people.

Improves Living Standards - Through production and trade, people access goods and services that enhance their quality of life.

In simple terms, economic activity is the "engine" that keeps the economy running, fueled by the work that people do and the things that they buy and sell.

Economic Data

Economic data refers to information and statistics that measure the performance and health of an economy. This data provides insight into how well an economy is functioning and helps individuals, businesses, and governments make informed decisions.

Examples of Economic Data

1. Gross Domestic Product (GDP) - Measures the total value of all goods and services produced in a country.

2. Employment Data - Tracks unemployment rates, job creation, and workforce participation.

3. Inflation Rates - This shows how the prices of goods and services change over time.

4. Consumer Spending - Indicates how much people are spending on goods and services.

5. Trade Data - Includes imports, exports, and trade balances.

6. Business Investment - Tracks how much businesses are spending on infrastructure, equipment, or innovation.

Why Is Economic Data Important?

Policy Making - Governments use economic data to set policies on taxes, spending, and interest rates.

Business Decisions - Companies rely on economic data to plan investments, manage resources, and forecast demand.

Personal Finance - Individuals use it to make decisions about spending, saving, and investing.

Economic Forecasting - Economists use data to predict future trends and identify potential risks or opportunities.

In short, economic data provides a snapshot of how an economy is performing and serves as a guide for decision-making across all levels of society.

The Importance of Understanding Economic Activity and Economic Data:

Being knowledgeable about Economic Activity and Economic Data is essential for the everyday person because it empowers them to make better decisions in the "game of life." Understanding these concepts allows individuals to navigate the financial and societal systems they are part of so that they can achieve greater stability and success.

These are Some Reasons Why Knowledge of Economic Activity and Data Matters:

1. Improved Financial Decisions

Understanding economic trends (e.g., inflation, interest rates) helps individuals make smarter choices about saving, investing, borrowing, and spending.

- For example, knowing that inflation is rising might encourage someone to save in ways that preserve purchasing power, like investing in assets that grow with inflation.

2. Job and Career Choices

Economic activity influences industries, job markets, and wages. Being aware of trends like automation or economic growth in certain sectors/industries can help people choose careers with stability and growth potential.

3. Protection Against Economic Risks

Knowledge of economic data (e.g., unemployment rates or recessions) helps people prepare for financial uncertainty, such as creating emergency funds or diversifying income sources.

4. Informed Voting and Civic Engagement

Economic policies affect taxes, healthcare, education, and wages. Being informed about economic activity helps individuals evaluate government decisions and advocate for policies that benefit them and their communities.

5. Better Business and Investment Decisions

Entrepreneurs and investors rely on economic data to assess risks and opportunities, like expanding a business during a growth period or avoiding sectors/industries struggling during economic downturns.

6. Understanding the Cost of Living

Economic activity directly impacts everyday life, from the prices of groceries to housing costs. Knowing what drives these changes allows individuals to adapt and plan accordingly.

In the "Game of Life," Why This Knowledge Is Power:

This Knowledge Provides a Strategic Advantage - Just like in any game, understanding the "rules" (economic forces) gives you an edge in managing resources and planning ahead.

This Knowledge Empowers Autonomy - Knowledge reduces dependence on others for advice or decision-making, fostering independence and confidence.

Autonomy is the ability to make your own decisions and act independently without being controlled by others. It can also refer to the state of being self-governing.

This Knowledge Strengthens Resilience - When people understand the economic forces around them, they are better equipped to *adapt to challenges, like rising costs or job market shifts.*

Ultimately, economic literacy allows people to actively participate in shaping their lives, rather than simply reacting to external forces, making it a critical skill in achieving success and security.

PART 2: PROSPERITY

Pt. 2 Chapter 1 Forever Growth plus Progress

Look at the Difference between the two!

	PROSPERING	SUCCEEDING
Definition	A state of flourishing, growth, and overall well-being in multiple aspects of life.	The accomplishment of a specific goal or objective.
Sustainability	Long-term and enduring, reflecting ongoing growth and fulfillment.	May be temporary or tied to a single achievement.
Measure of Success	Based on balance, fulfillment, and overall thriving in life.	Measured by the completion or attainment of a defined goal.
Emphasis	Focuses on living abundantly and cultivating a meaningful, flourishing life.	Focuses on achieving targets, whether personal, professional, or material.

PROSPERITY

PART 1

We live in a monetary system, so the need to generate income will always exist. Prosperity over merely making money is absolutely essential. As long as we depend on earning money to survive, we must have the right foundation and system in place to ensure that we can always generate new income.

Too many people get caught up in chasing a quick buck, thinking that if they just get a large lump sum of money, they'll be set for life. They believe money alone will solve their problems permanently, but they fail to realize one critical truth—<u>no amount of money lasts forever.</u>

<u>Life is an ongoing expense.</u> No matter how much you make today, you'll always need a way to generate income tomorrow. <u>But because people don't grasp this, they make decisions based on getting money *now*, even if it means compromising their integrity, dishonoring principles, or cutting corners just to secure the immediate gain.</u> In doing so, they often adopt a "get-over" mentality—taking shortcuts, burning bridges, and damaging relationships, all in the pursuit of short-term success.

<u>And the truth is, in the short run, they *do* succeed. They get the money. But they neglect the long-term consequences—the reputation they ruin, the customers they lose, the trust they destroy.</u> Eventually, they find themselves without a sustainable way to earn, stuck in a cycle of constantly chasing the next dollar instead of positioning themselves to attract wealth continuously.

That's why it's crucial to conduct business the right way—with integrity, strong morals, and honorable principles. Because as long as everything in this world costs a dollar, we'll always need to make a new dollar. And the key to staying financially stable isn't just *getting* money—it's building a foundation that ensures you'll *keep making* money as long as you participate within the game of life.

Therefore, the foundation *MUST BE* built on prospering, not just succeeding. Succeeding is about quick wins. Prospering is about long-term victories. <u>When you do good business, treat people right, and create lasting value, you build relationships and clientele that stand the test of time. And that's the true sustainable ingredients that foster financial freedom.</u>

PART 2

Money is the medium through which we access everything—food, shelter, transportation, healthcare, education, and even the tools we need to create more wealth. It's not just about personal expenses; it's the cost of survival and participation in society. Even if you paid off all your debts and had enough saved to live comfortably for years, time itself would erode your financial security because life's expenses never stop. Inflation increases the cost of living, unexpected emergencies arise, and new opportunities often require capital. <u>So, unless you've built a system that continuously generates income, you'll eventually find yourself back at square one, needing to make money again.</u>

That's why the key to financial stability isn't just about *getting* money. It's about building a foundation that ensures you'll *keep making* money continuously. Too many people focus on hitting a financial goal without thinking about sustainability. But real wealth isn't about how much money you *have* at the moment. Nor is it about the success of receiving "<u>sporadic paychecks.</u>" It's about how much money you can *keep generating* over time. The only way to maintain that is by building something that's designed to last. Whether it's a business with loyal customers, investments that grow, or skills that always keep you in demand or employed. <u>When you approach money with this mindset, you shift from chasing temporary success to</u>

establishing long-term prosperity. That's the difference between making money fast and making money *forever*.

A person who acquires $1 million, $10 million, or even $100 million in a single transaction, whether by luck, opportunity, or a single fortunate creation, may not be able to sustain their life as well as someone who has never made a million dollars at once but has a system that continuously generates income. Why? Because money runs out, but a system keeps producing. The person making less than $1,000 per paycheck, but earning consistently, is in a far stronger position than the one who had a big payday but no way to keep new money flowing in.

The reality is, it's only a matter of time before a sitting lump sum of money dries up. The expenses, inflation, bad decisions, and unforeseen circumstances will eat away at the money. But a person who has built a system, no matter how small the earnings seem at first, will always have income coming in. That's why you have to get your eyes off just wanting a big lump sum of money. Instead, focus on building something that lasts, something that ensures you always have a way to generate more.

Think about the person who hit the lottery, inherited a large sum of money, or even earned it—like ballplayers and entertainers who signed massive contracts. In that moment, they had what seemed like more than enough. But as time passed and the clock kept ticking, the truth became evident—the money was disappearing. And not before long, it was only a matter of time before they went completely broke. Not because they never had the money, but because they never had the knowledge or the discipline to sustain the money. But most importantly, they neglected to establish a system that would allow them to continuously generate new money throughout their lifetime.

That outcome is a direct result of a lack of understanding that true prosperity isn't found in a single payday. And because of this misunderstanding, a person may neglect establishing a system. They often overlook smaller streams of income simply because they don't grasp the power of continuous earnings over time.

The problem is, too many people look down on the smaller amounts of income while obsessing over the larger lump sums of money and big paydays. They chase the big payday because they don't understand the law of accumulation nor the process of planting a seed, watering it, and giving it time to grow. Ironically, they understand this concept in nature, but they fail to apply it to their finances.

Because of this, they never commit to the discipline and dedication required to work with what they have, no matter how small it seems. They dismiss "the smaller crumbs of money" instead of realizing that mastering the management of the smaller amounts of money is what prepares them for managing the larger sums of money. <u>Self-control, financial discipline, and proper money management are the real keys. Because even if their earnings start small, with consistency and smart decisions, those earnings will accumulate.</u> And once that money grows, they can then strategically invest to accelerate their financial growth.

But before any of that happens, they must first respect all amounts of money, the smaller amounts in addition to the larger amounts. The objective is to earn consistently.

Therefore, true prosperity lies in the system we put in place and the foundation we build to ensure we create <u>continual transactions</u> and <u>multiple acquisitions of wealth over time</u>. Without a system, money eventually runs out. But when we establish a structure that keeps generating income, we position ourselves for lasting financial security. This is why a system built on strong morals, great principles, and unwavering integrity is essential to ultimate success. Because when you do things the right way, you don't just make money—you create a legacy of prosperity that stands the test of time.

PART 3

  With the right character traits, principles, and discipline, we position ourselves to continuously take the necessary actions that lead to financial success. And with the right mindset, combined with the commitment to being habitual learners, we ensure that we are always growing within the game of life, rather than becoming stagnant. The biggest mistake people make is allowing their only focus to be on getting money—thinking, *"I just need to get some money, I just need to get some money."* And the truth is, with that kind of tunnel vision, they *might* get the money. But if the money is built on the wrong foundation, it won't last. If they lack the right characteristics, they may land on money—but they won't have the habits to keep making more money. And if they aren't dedicated to learning and evolving, they may get the money but find themselves stagnant, unsure of how to continue growing or expanding their success.

  Now, let's pause and reflect on what history has shown us. How many times have we seen people—from athletes to entertainers to entrepreneurs—who spent their entire focus on "trying to get the money" and then they actually achieved it? They got the big payday. They secured millions. But then, as we watched their behavior patterns, we saw the cracks in their foundation. Over time, many of them lost it all or ended up in financial ruin—not because they didn't make money, but because they never built the mindset, foundation nor system necessary to sustain it.

  And what's worse, some of them didn't even lose all their money, but they still ended up lost, directionless, and unfulfilled. They were victims of being stagnant at the top with money but no growth, no vision, and no clear purpose. In those cases, it may *look* like their problems stemmed from the fact that they accumulated too much money. But the accumulated money was never the problem. <u>The real issue was that their mindset wasn't structured for longevity,</u>

sustainability, or expansion. And because of that, even with all the money they accumulated, they were still at risk of falling.

This is why prospering is about more than just getting money. It's about establishing a system, a foundation, and the right habits that ensure financial growth over time. But beyond that, it's also about developing a mindset that keeps you learning, evolving, and expanding your knowledge. True prosperity isn't just about financial wealth—it's about constant mental growth, adaptability, and the discipline to keep improving. *Because money alone won't save you, but a system built with integrity, discipline, and a continually growing mindset will.*

So the reality is this—if we, as a people, and you and I, as individuals, neglect these fundamental principles, we are not just making a small mistake. In all actuality, we are neglecting, squandering, and discarding the very opportunity to build true generational wealth. Without these prosperous principles, we don't just risk losing money; we risk losing the legacy, the foundation, and the security that could have lasted for generations.

PART 4

To truly understand prosperity and prospering, we must recognize that being prosperous goes beyond just what works for us individually. We operate within a monetary system that requires exchange. It's a system where our financial well-being is directly connected to the financial well-being of others.

Prospering isn't about hoarding all the money for yourself. It's about understanding the flow of money within the system. In order for you to make money, someone else has to spend money with you. And for someone else to spend money with you, they must first have money to spend. That means prosperity isn't just about you making all the money. Because in order for you to prosper financially, money must be in circulation throughout the entire game of life.

You need money, and so do the other participants in the system. And in reality, you actually need other people to have money, because if they don't, who will buy from you? Just as they need money to spend with you, you also need money to spend with them. This mutual exchange is what keeps the system flowing, which is why true prosperity isn't just about getting money. It's about ensuring that money continues to circulate in a way that benefits everyone involved within the game-of-life.

In alignment with the factors that drive the circulation of money within the game of life, you and I have the ability to generate income—whether it's small amounts or large sums. The opportunity to earn money exists for those who understand and apply the principles that keep money flowing. Because there's more than enough in circulation.

But generating income is only the first step. After making money, we must also understand the laws that govern our cash flow—how money moves, how to manage it effectively, and how to keep it working for us instead of simply spending it until it's gone. Because without a proper system to not only generate income but also manage and grow it, even the most consistent earnings can be lost to poor financial habits, bad investments, and lack of foresight.

Once we master these fundamental elements, we begin to truly understand the value of someone spending money with us—and us spending money with the next person. Whether that next person is a loved one, a friend, a neighbor, someone within our community, society, or even our nation, the circulation of money plays a crucial role in everyone's financial well-being.

When someone spends money with you or me—whether by employing us, patronizing our business, or investing in what we offer—they are not just making a transaction. What they are really doing is helping us sustain life, cover essential expenses, and achieve "step one" in the financial growth and generational wealth-building process. "Step one" is always to generate income.

On the flip side, when you help someone else generate income, whether through employment or supporting their business, you're actually helping them achieve the same financial stability and progress that you seek when money is spent with you. And you're helping them achieve "step one" as well. This is why the circulation of money is just as important as the obtaining of money. Because prosperity isn't just about the individual, it's about the collective.

True prosperity isn't just about what "I do, he does, or she does." It's about what "WE DO" together. When we embrace and apply this understanding to our contributions to society, we unlock the full power of financial growth, sustainability, and long-term wealth; not just individually, but collectively.

PART 5

Think about the process of a system that produces plants. Before there is a thriving garden, there must first be a seed. That seed needs soil to be planted in. Then, it requires essential elements like water and sunlight to grow. When all of these elements are properly aligned, we get a beautiful, flourishing garden filled with strong, thriving plants.

Now, compare that system to yourself within the game of life. In order for you to thrive, you also need essential elements. You need other people who play different roles within society. You need resources, opportunities, and financial circulation that keep the system moving. Just like plants need the right conditions to grow, we, as people, need a healthy flow of money between individuals, businesses, and communities so that everyone has a chance to grow and prosper.

The challenge is that sometimes we don't see how all these different elements—industries, people, and resources—connect to our personal well-being. We become so accustomed to only seeing the world we were born into—our neighborhood, our immediate surroundings—that we struggle to recognize the larger system at play. But whether we see it or not, life is a vast interconnected game, stretching far beyond what our eyes can perceive. And within this game, every participant—whether visible to us or not—plays a role in the well-being of one another.

So believe me when I say, we need each other. And we don't just need each other to exist. We need each other to function at our best. Because when I am operating at my best, when my loved ones, my friends, my neighbors, and my community are all functioning at their best, we move closer to creating a society that is operating at its best. And when one society prospers, and another society prospers, we build a nation that prospers

But achieving collective prosperity starts with one individual—just like a single seed is the beginning of an entire garden. If just one individual commits to building a strong foundation rooted in the laws of prosperity, <u>it helps create a prosperous world for us all.</u>

A world of prosperous individuals creates a prosperous society. And multiple prosperous societies create a prosperous world. But it all starts with you and me—choosing to function, operate, and build upon the right principles. If I commit to it, if you commit to it, and if our communities commit to it, then we take one step closer to existing in a world where prosperity isn't just possible—it will be the foundation of how we live.

PART 6

If an individual neglects or goes against the foundation of prosperity, they aren't just harming themselves—they're contributing to the destruction of others as well. Just like pollution damages the environment, making it harder for plants to grow, bad financial habits, unethical actions, and short-term thinking pollute the economic and social system we all depend on. When one person fails to uphold integrity, discipline, and proper financial management, they don't just stagnate their own growth—they make it harder for others to thrive, <u>weakening the very foundation that sustains us all.</u>

But just as a plant is designed to sustain and maintain life even after experiencing moments of pollution, you, as a human being, possess the supreme capability to establish and maintain a prosperous foundation—regardless of the challenges around you. *<u>You are constructed to exemplify strength, resilience, and a strong will.</u>*

So if someone else pollutes your environment with inequality, unethical practices, short-term thinking, or bad financial habits, understand that you are built to overcome it all. <u>No external force—no circumstance, no setback, no negativity—can permanently stop you unless you allow it to.</u>

The power to thrive is in your hands. If you dedicate yourself to the right principles, the right mindset, and the right characteristics, and if you lay the right foundation, then the fruits from a prosperous tree will forever feed you. *Because prosperity isn't just about what happens around you.* <u>*It's about what you cultivate within yourself.*</u>

When I say "*<u>it's about what you cultivate within yourself,</u>*" I mean that your success, prosperity, and ability to thrive start from within you—your mindset, your discipline, your principles, and your actions. <u>*No matter what happens around you, it's the qualities you develop and strengthen inside yourself that determine whether you will succeed or struggle.*</u>

"Cultivate" means to develop, grow, or nurture something over time with care and intention—just like a farmer cultivates crops by planting seeds, watering them, and ensuring they have the right conditions to grow.

Cultivating prosperity and personal growth means:

- <u>Developing the right mindset</u>—a mindset focused on long-term success, discipline, and integrity.
- <u>Strengthening your character</u>—so you remain resilient despite challenges.
- <u>Building financial wisdom</u>—so you manage money wisely and create a system for continuous income.
- <u>Practicing good habits consistently</u>—so success becomes a natural result of how you live.

So when I say "*<u>it's about what you cultivate within yourself</u>*," I mean that prosperity doesn't just come from external factors like luck or opportunities. It comes from who you become, what you build internally, and how you position yourself to succeed, <u>regardless of your circumstances.</u>

<u>Your environment may challenge you, but if you cultivate the right principles, skills, and mindset, you'll always find a way to prosper.</u>

We must acknowledge a critical reality. When a community or neighborhood appears to be in ruin or faces extreme challenges, <u>many believe that the environment itself is the problem.</u> As a result, the most common solution people turn to is the idea of moving to a new community, under the belief that by changing their environment, they are escaping the issues that existed in their previous neighborhood.

However, what we often fail to realize is that our communities and neighborhoods are built on land. And the land itself is not the problem. The community and neighborhood that exists on top of the land are not the issue. The true issue is <u>the lack of prosperity-driven principles</u> being practiced by the people living there.

Therefore, if we truly desire a prosperous world and hope to live in thriving communities, the solution does not start with relocating. It starts with cultivating and exercising prosperous qualities from within ourselves first.

So, as we move forward in instilling prosperous qualities, such as principles tied to strong character, financial discipline, and integrity—we will, over time, systematically produce prosperous people, who then create and sustain prosperous communities. Just as a farmer produces a thriving land by cultivating prosperous crops, we must cultivate prosperity within ourselves to transform the environments we live in.

The power of prosperity doesn't just lie in the hands of fate. It lies in the hands, the mindset, the character, and the actions of you and I. It's in the principles we practice, the discipline we uphold, and the foundation we build.

So let's commit. Let's build. Let's grow. And then let's experience growth on top of growth, on top of growth, on top of growth. Because prosperity isn't given—it's created. And it starts with us, and it will continue with those who mimic our prosperous characteristics.

Pt. 2 Chapter 2
Respect The Game

Learn The Game,
Move with the Wisdom of How
The Game Is Structured
&
Let that Knowledge Be One
of the Keys to Your Prosperity

LIFE IS THE GAME

Let's start with the truth: this world we're living in is a game, and the structure of modern society is what forms the playing field that we now recognize as the game of life. This game of life is like a sport of its own. And just like any other sport, this game comes with *an objective, a set of rules, participants,* and *officials who govern the play*.

In sports, the objective might be to score points, win a championship, or outperform the opponent. While in the game of life, the objective is often centered around the pursuit of generating income, building stability, creating freedom, and establishing a legacy. But no matter what the objective is, every player must understand the rules. Because understanding the rules is just as important as understanding the objective of the game.

Think about it: when you're playing basketball, football, or soccer, there are rules that must be followed. You don't always know who wrote the rules, and you may not agree with them. But you respect the rules, because you understand that they govern how the game is played.

And when you think about it in a deeper sense, every sport has a referee. And the referee's job is to govern the game. Their job is to enforce the rules. The rules that they enforce are rules that come from a rulebook. And the rulebook is structured by the rule makers. And truthfully, you may never meet the people who created the rulebook, but their influence shows up every time the referee blows the whistle. And if you go against the rules or disregard the orders of the referee, you will be met with penalties. And if you accumulate too many penalties, you will be benched. And if you channel your aggression of frustration towards the ref, you may get ejected from the game.

Now, let's bring that concept to the reality of the real world. The truth of the matter is that you and I are the participants within this game of life. And the rules are the laws, the policies, and the systems that have been established by politicians, lawmakers, and executives—which are the rule makers. And the referees in life are the police officers, lawyers, judges, and enforcers whose job is to keep order and ensure that the game is being played according to the established structure and rule book.

And just like in any sport, if you go against the rules or you fight the referees, you become subject to the penalties. But in the real world, the penalties may be incarceration, financial struggles, restricted freedom, or lost opportunities.

But the beautiful part is this: If you learn the rules and you play the game effectively, you can master the game. You can rise through the ranks. You can build your position. You can gain influence, wealth, and power. And once you're in a position of power, you can help change the rules. You can shift policies, propose laws, and bring fairness to the playing field—not just for yourself but for everyone who plays the game after you. This is the real definition of legacy.

True prosperity in this game comes from understanding the system, navigating it wisely, and rising high enough to influence it. It's about discipline, strategy, character, and purpose. When you learn how to move with wisdom, stay grounded, and execute with vision, *you don't just remain a participant within the game; you rise to become one of the forces that shape it.*

It's fair to say that, at times, the rules of the game don't feel fair. But here's the reality: *"<u>YOU'RE STILL IN THE GAME.</u>"* So, neglecting the rules won't help you. Disobeying the rules won't help you. Rebelling against the rules and refusing to gain an understanding of the system won't help you. That behavior pattern will only put you at a greater disadvantage within the game.

One of the greatest things you can do is learn the rules, learn the game, and then play the game wisely. Your results will only equal out to greatness when you participate as an individual armed with supreme intelligence, the right mindset, the right characteristics and a strong foundation of principles.

From there, you will gain the power to take control of your reality *within* this game. And more than that, you will also gain the power to impact the reality of others within this game as well.

So, with that being said, that's how you move from surviving to thriving and from a player to a leader. *"THIS IS HOW YOU CHANGE THE GAME FROM THE INSIDE OUT!"*

SO ONCE AGAIN, LEARN THE GAME; RESPECT THE GAME; AND PLAY THE GAME ACCORDINGLY!

PART 3: BUILDING STRONG CHARACTER

The Importance of Parts 3 & 4

In the process of embedding principles within our children, it's not enough to just tell them what values like integrity, discipline, or humility mean. <u>We have to make these words identifiable in real life</u>. Just like a child watching basketball can recognize a foul, a double dribble, or a layup, they should also be able to recognize determination, accountability, and consistency in the world around them.

This is why Part 2 and Part 3 are structured the way they are.

1) First, our children must become aware of these words. "They need to hear them, see them, and recognize their importance."

2) Next, they need to understand what these words mean. "Definitions bring clarity and give these words structure."

3) Finally, they need to learn how to identify these traits within actions. "Whether it's in the actions of themselves or others, they should be able to observe behavior, recognize the qualities behind it, and name what they see."

The goal is to give our children the same level of awareness for character traits as they have for the rules of a sport. Just as they can call an offside in football or an interception, they should be able to recognize when someone is displaying resilience, when someone lacks accountability, or when integrity is being tested.

This ability to SEE and NAME these traits will not only help them navigate life but will also help them refine their own behavior. Because when you can put a name to an action, you can better understand it, learn from it, and either embody it or correct it.

<u>This is what makes instilling these principles truly effective</u>— by not just teaching these values but <u>making them something our children can recognize, relate to, and apply in their everyday lives.</u>

It's not just about memorizing definitions; it's about RECOGNITION and APPLICATION, which will assist in making the lessons stick.

Pt. 3 Chapter 1
Humility

Let's Look into the Word "Humility"

Humble:

Being humble is the way you act when you have humility.

If you're humble, you don't brag about your achievements or try to make others feel small.

Instead, you show respect for others, listen to their ideas, and appreciate them.

Modest:

Being modest means not showing off or acting like you're better than everyone else,

even if you've done something really great.

It's about keeping a balanced view of yourself and staying chill about your achievements.

Being modest can also mean not dressing or acting in a way that's designed to grab all the attention.

For instance,

Wearing something simple rather than something super flashy or over-the-top is considered modest.

In short:

Being modest means staying humble and respectful and not making everything about you.

It's a way to be confident without being cocky.

For example,

if you get a good grade on a test, a modest/humble person might say,

"I studied hard, but the teacher explained it well,"

instead of, "Yeah, I'm just smarter than everyone else."

It's not about hiding your success—it's just not rubbing it in other people's faces.

Humility Definition:

Humility is the state of being humble!

"Humility" is the quality of having a modest/humble view of your own importance.

It involves being honest about your strengths and weaknesses, recognizing that

you don't know everything, and valuing others' perspectives without arrogance or pride.

Humility is about staying grounded, being open to learning, and treating

others with respect, regardless of your achievements or status.

The Mindset of Humility:

Humility is a mindset or attitude. It's about how you see yourself and others.

If you have humility, you understand that you're not

perfect, and you don't think you're better than anyone else

no matter how talented, smart, or successful you are.

You also don't put others down to make yourself feel better.

Instead, you're open to learning from people, admitting

when you're wrong, and giving credit where it's due.

It's about being honest with yourself and knowing your strengths without letting them make you feel "above" others and being okay with learning and growing

(while being aware of your weaknesses without feeling bad about them.).

Think of humility as being confident but not arrogant.

For example,

If you score the winning goal in a soccer game, someone with humility might say,

"It was a team effort," instead of, "Yeah, I'm the best

on the field." It's about staying grounded and respecting everyone, including yourself.

How Humility Allows You To Grow:

(& Remain a Student of Life For a Lifetime)

Humility in learning means being open to the fact that you don't know everything—and that's okay.

It's about having the mindset that there's always more to discover, more to understand, and more ways to grow.

It's what helps you stay curious and willing to listen to others, no matter how smart or experienced you already are.

When you approach learning with humility, you:

1. Admit you don't know everything:

This is important because it opens the door to growth.

If you think you already know it all, you won't feel the need to learn anything new.

2. Ask questions:

Being humble means you're not afraid to ask for help or clarification.

You know it's not about looking smart; it's about understanding.

3. Listen to others:

Even if someone has less experience than you, you stay open to their ideas.

They might see things differently or share something valuable that you never considered.

4. Accept mistakes:

Humility helps you see mistakes as part of learning, not something to be ashamed of.

It's a chance to improve, not a failure.

For example,

Imagine you're learning how to play guitar.

If you have humility, you're okay with struggling at first, listening to your

teacher's advice, and practicing over and over without feeling embarrassed.

You know there's always more to learn, even if you've mastered a few chords.

In short:

Humility in learning is what helps you stay teachable.

It reminds you that everyone is always a work in progress, and that's what makes life interesting!

Pt. 3 Chapter 2
Integrity

Let's Look into the Word "Integrity"

Ethics:

Ethics is like a set of rules that help people decide what's right and wrong in life.

Morals:

Morals are the specific rules or beliefs about what is right and wrong that guide how you behave.

Principle:

Principles are the basic beliefs or rules that guide how you think, behave, or make

decisions.

They act like a compass, helping you decide what's right or wrong in different situations.

The Difference between "Ethics, Morals, and Principles:

The words ethics, morals, and principles are related, but they're not the same.

Think of them as different layers of understanding what's "right" and "wrong." Here's the difference:

1. Ethics

- What it means: Ethics are rules about how people should behave in a group, society, or job.

These rules aren't about what you feel but about what's agreed upon by everyone within that system of established rules or guidelines.

- These are the specific "do's and don'ts" for how you should behave.

- Where they come from: They come from outside of you—like from laws, school rules, or professional codes.

- How they work: They help people work together and avoid chaos.

- Example: If you're a doctor, ethics tell you to keep patients' secrets (confidentiality) and always do what's best for them.

2. Morals

- What it means: Morals are your personal beliefs about what's right and wrong.

These come from inside you and are shaped by how you were raised, what you believe in, or your life experiences.

- These are the specific "do's and don'ts" for how you should behave.
- Where they come from: Your family, religion, culture, or what feels right to you.
- How they work: They guide your personal choices, even if no one else agrees with you.
- Example: You might believe that lying is always wrong, even if everyone else thinks it's okay in certain situations.

3. Principles

- What it means: Principles are big, basic ideas that help you decide what to do in any situation.

They're like a guidebook for life. They're not about specific rules but about the big picture.

- These are the big ideas or beliefs that explain why those rules exist.
- Where they come from: Logical thinking or lessons you've learned in life.
- How they work: They're like a compass that helps you stay on track with what you believe is fair or right.
- Example: A principle like "treat others how you want to be treated" can guide you in all kinds of situations—at school, home, or with friends.

In short:

- Ethics is about societal or professional rules.
- Morals are about personal rules/values.
- Principles are foundational ideas that guide both ethics and morals. It's Like the Mentality that Guides the RULES.

How They're Different

Here's an easy way to remember:

1. Ethics: Rules set by a group or society.
- Think: "This is what's expected of everyone."

2. Morals: Your own personal beliefs.
- Think: "This is what I believe."

3. Principles: Big ideas that guide everything.
- Think: "This is the foundation of what's right."

Quick Examples

- Ethics: Your teacher tells you not to cheat because it's against the school's rules.
- Morals: You personally believe that cheating is wrong, even if you wouldn't get caught.
- Principle: You think fairness is important, so you wouldn't cheat because it's unfair to others.

The Big Difference:

- Principles are the why behind your actions.
- Morals are what you do because of those principles.

It's like this: principles are the big picture, and morals are the specific rules that help you follow that picture.

The Difference Between Ethical & Moral:

Ethical:

Being ethical means knowing the difference between what's right and wrong and choosing to do what's right.

It's about following rules, being fair, and treating others with respect, even when it's hard or no one is watching.

Moral:

Being Moral means knowing the difference between right and wrong and choosing to do what's right.

It's like a personal guide for how you behave and make decisions in life.

Here's an example:

Imagine you find a wallet with money inside of it on the ground, and you decide to return it instead of keeping the money.

That's an ethical choice because it's the right thing to do.

That's a moral choice because it's the right thing to do.

Being ethical is about doing the right thing, not just because you have to, but because you know it's the right thing to do.

And being moral is about sticking to what's right, even when it's hard or when no one is looking!

Being Moral & Ethical In Business:

(Being Moral) & (Being Ethical) means making decisions that are fair, honest, and good for everyone involved—not just focused on making money.

For Example:

- Being honest with customers about a product's flaws is a moral/ethical decision.

Good Morals, Ethics, and Principles in Business:

Good morals, ethics, and principles are essential for business because they create trust, build a positive reputation, and help the business succeed in the long run.

Here's how they work together to benefit a company:

1. Good Morals in Business

Morals are the specific right and wrong actions a business chooses to take.

Acting with good morals means treating people fairly, honestly, and kindly.

- Why it's good for business:
- Customers trust and support businesses that act morally (e.g., being honest about product quality).
- Employees feel respected and are more motivated to work hard.
- Example: A company refuses to cheat customers or underpay workers, even if it could make more money.

2. Ethics in Business

Ethics is the overall system of rules that helps a business decide how to act in a fair and responsible way.

- Why it's good for business:
- Ethical businesses avoid scandals, lawsuits, and bad press.
- It builds a company's reputation as one people want to buy from or work for.

- Example: A business that avoids harmful practices, like dumping waste into rivers, shows it cares about the environment and society.

3. Principles in Business

Principles are the big ideas or values that guide a business's decisions, like fairness, integrity, and respect.

They act as the company's moral compass.

- Why it's good for business:
- They create consistency, so the business always behaves in a way people can trust.
- They help the business make tough decisions by sticking to what's important.
- Example: A company with the principle of "honesty" won't hide bad news from investors or customers.

How They Help Businesses Succeed:

1. Customer Loyalty:

- When a business acts with good morals, ethics, and principles, customers trust it and keep coming back.

2. Employee Satisfaction:

- Workers are happier and more productive when they know their company is doing the right thing.

3. Reputation:

- A business that is known for being fair and ethical attracts more customers, partners, and investors.

4. Avoiding Problems:

- Unethical actions might work in the short term, but they lead to scandals, fines, or a bad reputation in the long run.

Example of All Three at Work:

A company that believes in fairness (principle) ensures its employees are paid fairly (moral) and follows labor laws (ethics).

This attracts good workers and customers who want to support a business that cares.

In short, having good morals, ethics, and principles isn't just the right thing to do—it's also smart for long-term success in business!

Integrity:

Integrity is about being honest, reliable, and doing the right thing, even when it's hard or no one is watching.

It's like being the kind of person others can always count on because they know you'll stick to your word and treat them fairly.

Integrity in Business:

In business, integrity is super important because it builds trust.

Imagine you're running a business, and you always deal honestly with your customers—if something goes wrong, you own up to it and fix it.

People will respect that and keep coming back to you.

Employees also want to work for a boss or company that's fair and doesn't cut corners.

On the flip side, if a business lies or cheats, it won't take long for people to stop supporting it.

Integrity helps a business grow because it creates strong relationships with customers, employees, and partners.

When people trust you, they're more likely to stick with you, recommend you to others, and help your business grow and succeed.

In short, integrity is like a strong foundation.

Without it, everything falls apart.

But with it, people trust you, and trust is everything in life and in business.

Key aspects of integrity include:

- Honesty: Speaking and acting truthfully.

- Accountability: Taking responsibility for your actions and their consequences.

- Consistency: Demonstrating reliability in upholding principles across different situations.

- Moral Courage: Doing the right thing, even in the face of opposition or risk.

Integrity is often considered a cornerstone of trustworthiness and respect in personal, professional, and social contexts.

Pt. 3 Chapter 3
Discipline

Let's Look into the Word "Discipline"

Discipline in relation to succeeding:

Discipline along the journey of success is the consistent application of effort, focus, and self-control to achieve long-term goals, even in the face of challenges, distractions, or temporary setbacks.

It is the backbone of progress, enabling individuals to stay aligned with their vision and push through obstacles.

Key Aspects of Discipline on the Journey to Success:

1. Commitment to Routine

Success often requires a daily commitment to productive habits—whether practicing a skill, learning, or working on a project.

Discipline ensures that small and consistent actions compound into significant results over time.

2. Delayed Gratification

Discipline involves prioritizing long-term goals over immediate pleasures.

This might mean sacrificing leisure, resisting distractions, or investing time and energy into activities that yield results later.

3. Focus on Priorities

Along the journey, distractions and competing demands will arise.

Discipline keeps you focused on what truly matters, helping you allocate your time and energy effectively.

4. Resilience in Adversity

Discipline fuels persistence when the journey gets tough.

It helps you maintain momentum during failures, setbacks, or discouragement, reminding you that growth comes from overcoming challenges.

5. Consistency Over Motivation

Motivation can waver, but discipline ensures that action is taken regardless of how you feel.

It's about showing up and doing the work, even on days when enthusiasm is low.

6. Self-Control and Accountability

Discipline requires managing impulses, staying accountable for your decisions, and avoiding shortcuts that compromise the integrity of your goals.

7. Continuous Improvement

Success requires learning from failures and seeking growth.

Discipline helps you commit to lifelong learning and adaptability, ensuring you improve as you progress.

Examples of Discipline in Practice:

*Waking up early to work toward personal goals before starting your day job.

*Sticking to a financial budget to save for a business or investment.

* Practicing a skill every day, even when progress feels slow.

*Saying no to distractions like excessive social media use or unnecessary social obligations.

*Taking responsibility for mistakes and staying focused on solutions.

Discipline transforms ambition into action and potential into achievement.

It's the steady engine that powers the long, often difficult, but ultimately rewarding journey to success.

Discipline in relation to Self-Control:

Discipline in relation to self-control is the ability to regulate your thoughts, emotions, and behaviors to align with your long-term goals and values.

It is a form of self-mastery where you resist temptations, distractions, or impulses that could derail your progress, choosing instead to act in a way that supports your aspirations.

Key Elements of Discipline and Self-Control:

1. Impulse Management

Discipline requires self-control to pause and evaluate before acting on an impulse.

Whether it's resisting unhealthy food, avoiding unnecessary spending, or refraining from emotional reactions, self-control ensures that immediate desires don't override better judgment.

2. Sticking to Priorities

Discipline helps you focus on what matters most, while self-control ensures you don't deviate when faced with short-term temptations or distractions that offer no real value.

3. Overcoming Procrastination

Discipline, fueled by self-control, combats the urge to delay tasks. It pushes you to take action even when you don't feel like

it, keeping momentum toward your goals.

4. Emotional Regulation

Self-control is key to managing emotions like frustration, anger, or discouragement.

Discipline uses this regulation to maintain composure and stay productive, even under pressure.

5. Delayed Gratification

Self-control enables you to prioritize future rewards over immediate pleasures, while discipline ensures you consistently act on that principle.

This combination allows for progress in areas like saving money, building skills, or achieving fitness goals.

6. Consistency

Discipline relies on self-control to establish and maintain habits.

By controlling urges to skip workouts, cut corners, or quit, you build the consistency needed for lasting success.

Practical Examples of Discipline and Self-Control in Action:

*Choosing to study or work on a project instead of binge-watching a show.

*Maintaining a calm and professional tone in a heated discussion.

*Sticking to a fitness plan when tempted by unhealthy options.

*Saving money instead of making impulse purchases.

*Waking up early despite the desire to stay in bed.

Relationship Between the Two:

"Self-control" is the moment-to-moment decision to act in line with your values.

"Discipline" is the overarching framework of habits, routines, and commitments that guide those decisions.

Together, discipline and self-control enable you to stay on course, overcome obstacles, and build a life that reflects your best self.

Discipline in Relation to a Strong-Mind:

Discipline, in relation to having a strong mind, is the mental fortitude to stay focused, resilient, and consistent in pursuing goals, even when faced with challenges, temptations, or discomfort.

It reflects the ability to control thoughts and emotions, channeling them toward productive actions rather than allowing them to derail progress.

Key Aspects of Discipline and a Strong Mind:

1. Mental Resilience

A strong mind, powered by discipline, helps you bounce back from failures, setbacks, or criticism.

Discipline keeps you grounded and motivated to continue working toward your goals despite difficulties.

2. Focus and Clarity

Discipline sharpens mental focus, allowing you to ignore distractions and concentrate on what truly matters.

A strong mind uses discipline to prioritize goals and maintain clarity even in chaotic situations.

3. Emotional Control

A disciplined mind can regulate emotions like fear, frustration, or doubt.

Instead of being overwhelmed, it channels these emotions into positive action or learning opportunities.

4. Consistency Under Pressure

A strong mind doesn't waver under stress or adversity.

Discipline ensures consistency in your efforts and decisions, even when circumstances become challenging or uncertain.

5. Mastery of Impulses

Discipline, tied to mental strength, allows you to overcome immediate urges or desires that conflict with your long-term goals.

It's the strength to say "no" when necessary and stick to your commitments.

6. Positive Self-Talk

A disciplined mind replaces negative or self-defeating thoughts with constructive ones.

This helps you stay motivated and confident, reinforcing the belief that success is achievable.

7. Growth Mindset

Discipline supports a strong mind by fostering a commitment to lifelong learning and improvement.

It enables you to embrace challenges as opportunities to grow rather than as obstacles.

Practical Examples of Discipline and a Strong Mind:

*Persisting on a difficult task instead of giving up when it feels overwhelming.

*Staying calm and focused during high-stress situations.

*Practicing mindfulness to control negative or distracting thoughts.

*Adhering to a routine, such as exercising or journaling, even when motivation is low.

*Choosing to face fears or uncertainties with courage instead of avoiding them.

The Connection:

A "Strong Mind is the foundation of discipline, providing the mental strength to stay committed and focused.

Discipline, in turn, reinforces mental strength by building habits and actions that align with your goals and values.

Together, they create a powerful synergy that drives success and personal growth.

Pt. 3 Chapter 4 Accountability

Let's Look into the Word "Accountability"

Accountability:

Accountability means taking responsibility for what you do and owning the results of your choices, whether the results are good or bad. It's about being honest with yourself and others.

Accountability is the obligation or willingness to accept responsibility for one's actions, decisions, and outcomes.

It's like saying, "I'm in charge of my actions and how they affect my life and the lives of others."

Being honest with yourself is at the heart of accountability. It means looking at your actions, decisions, and habits with complete clarity, without making excuses or ignoring uncomfortable truths. This self-honesty allows you to recognize both - your strengths and areas where you need to grow, which is essential for personal development.

When you're honest with yourself, you can no longer blame others or external circumstances for your situation. Instead, you acknowledge your role in what's happening in your life.

For example, if you're struggling with a goal, being honest might mean admitting that you've been procrastinating or not putting in enough effort rather than claiming it's because "life is too hard" or "someone else held you back."

This kind of accountability creates a powerful sense of self-awareness. It helps you align your actions with your goals and values, giving you the ability to make better choices.

Ultimately, being honest with yourself is liberating—it gives you control over your life because you're no longer hiding from the truth or waiting for external forces to change things for you.

Accountability, in the context of the first step of self-improvement, refers to taking full ownership of your current state, actions, and choices without deflecting blame onto external factors. It is the conscious acknowledgment that your growth begins with accepting responsibility for your life and the outcomes you've experienced so far.

This foundational step requires honesty with yourself—admitting your strengths and weaknesses, recognizing habits that hinder progress, and understanding the role your decisions play in shaping your reality. By doing so, you position yourself to take intentional action toward change, as you are no longer waiting for external circumstances to shift but are actively taking charge of your journey.

Accountability empowers self-improvement by fostering discipline, self-awareness, and a commitment to personal growth.

In Addition:

It involves being answerable to oneself or others for fulfilling commitments, meeting expectations, or correcting mistakes when necessary. Accountability is often associated with transparency, integrity, and a proactive attitude toward resolving issues and achieving goals, keeping your promises, and fixing things when you mess up.

Being accountable shows you're mature, reliable, and ready to handle life's challenges.

Pt. 3 Chapter 5 Gratitude

Let's Look into the Word "Gratitude"

Gratitude:

Gratitude can be defined as a deep, conscious acknowledgment and appreciation for the opportunities, experiences, and potential that life offers—particularly the chance to grow, learn, and create meaning for oneself. It is an attitude of recognizing the inherent and priceless value of being alive and embracing the possibilities within each moment, even amidst challenges.

It is the conscious choice to appreciate life, emphasizing both appreciation for what is and hope for what can be.

1. Being Grateful for Life

Life is a unique and unpredictable journey. Gratitude in this context means recognizing the miracle of simply being here, alive, and present. It's about embracing each breath, heartbeat, and moment as an opportunity to engage with the world.

- This kind of gratitude fosters a sense of humility and reverence for existence, reminding us that life, with all its imperfections, is still a privilege.

2. The Opportunity to Make Something of Yourself

Gratitude for personal growth acknowledges that every day brings new chances to define who you are. It's the understanding that challenges and setbacks are not just obstacles but also stepping stones to resilience and wisdom.

- By being thankful for the ability to shape your own path, you foster motivation and positivity, which can help you to persevere in your goals and aspirations.

3. The Opportunity to Learn Something New

Gratitude for learning reflects an appreciation for the mind's capacity to grow. It means cherishing the fact that, no matter where you are in life, you can still acquire knowledge, develop skills, and gain new perspectives.

- This mindset turns curiosity into a celebration and transforms even mistakes into valuable lessons.

"The Bigger Picture"

Gratitude ties all these elements together by shifting your focus from what is lacking to what is possible. It creates a foundation for contentment and ambition to coexist. When you combine being grateful for life with an appreciation for growth and learning, you cultivate a mindset that sees challenges as opportunities and each day as a chance to become a better version of yourself.

Living with gratitude doesn't mean ignoring hardships but rather choosing to focus on the opportunities within times of experiencing hardship. It's a mindset that opens doors to fulfillment, resilience, and lasting joy.

PART 4: THE INGREDIENTS TO SUCCESS

Pt. 4 Chapter 1 Mindset

IMPULSE:

Impulse is when you do something suddenly, without thinking it through or planning it.

It's like your brain says, "Just do it!" before you stop to ask yourself if it's a good idea or not.

What does impulse look like?

1. Acting on feelings

Impulses are driven by emotions, like excitement, anger, or even boredom, without stopping to think about the consequences.

- Example: You're mad at a friend, so you send them a mean text right away. That's acting on impulse, and later, you might regret it.

2. Quick decisions without planning

Acting on Impulse is when you skip the step of thinking logically or weighing the pros and cons.

- Example: You see a new video game at the store, so you spend all your money on it without considering if you'll need that money for something else later.

Why is it essential to understand impulse?

- It helps you avoid mistakes

Acting on impulse can lead to decisions you regret, like saying something hurtful or spending money you were saving for something important.

-It helps with big decisions

Thinking things through can save you from much trouble.

Example of impulse vs. thinking it through:

"Impulse" Your friend dares you to skip class, and you do it without thinking about the consequences, like getting in trouble.

"Thinking it through": You pause and realize that skipping class might seem fun now, but it'll mess up your grades or get you grounded.

In simple terms, impulse is when you act without thinking, like hitting "go" before checking if it's the right move.

It's normal to feel impulses, but learning to pause and think first can help you make smarter choices.

LOGIC:

Logic is a way of thinking that helps you figure out if something makes sense or is true. It's like a tool your brain uses to connect ideas and understand how things work. Logic is about thinking in a way that makes sense, following rules, facts, and evidence.

Here's an Example:

Imagine someone tells you, "All cats like milk. This animal is a cat. So, it likes milk." That's logical because the idea follows a clear pattern:

1. All cats like milk (fact).

2. This is a cat (fact).

3. Therefore, this cat likes milk (Is a Logical conclusion. Because the conclusion is based around FACTS.)

But if someone said, "All cats like milk. This animal is a dog. So, it likes milk," you'd know that's "not logical" because the facts don't match up.

(The conclusion IS NOT based around FACTS)

Why Logic Matters:

1) Logic helps you weigh your options and choose what makes the most sense.

2) Logic can help you tell when something doesn't add up.

3) Logic helps you find solutions step by step.

REASON:

Reason is your ability to think clearly and figure things out using logic and facts. It's like a mental tool you use to make sense of the world, solve problems, and make good decisions.

Think of it this way: when you use reason, you're not just going with your feelings or guessing—you're carefully thinking things through to find the most logical answer or solution.

How Reason Works:

1. Asking "Why?" and "How?"

- Reason helps you ask questions to understand things better.

For example, instead of just accepting, "That's how it is," you ask, "Why is it like that? Does it make sense?"

2. Connecting the Dots

- You use reason to see how things are related.

3. Checking for Truth

- Reason helps you figure out what's true and what's not by looking at evidence.

For example, if someone tells you something unbelievable, reason helps you think, "Does this match what I know? Do I need proof before I believe it?"

4. Solving Problems

- Reason helps you work through tough situations. Instead of freaking out, you think, "What's the problem? What are my options? What's the best solution?"

In short, reason is like your brain's superpower. It helps you stop, think, and make sense of things so you can make better choices and live a more thoughtful life.

Reason & Logic:

The difference between "reason" and "logic" is this:

- Logic is the "set of rules" or the system that helps you think clearly and make sense of things. It's like the structure or blueprint for good thinking.

- Reason is when you use those rules in your everyday life to figure things out, solve problems, or make decisions. It's the actual process of thinking logically.

An Easy Way to Understand It:

Think of logic as the instructions for building something, like a Lego set.

Reason is you following those instructions to actually build the thing.

They work together—logic gives you the tools, and reason is how you use them.

Why Both Are Good for Your Journey in Life:

- "Logic" shows you how to weigh facts and make choices that make sense.
- "Reason" helps you think through those choices in real-life situations.

- Life is full of challenges.

Using reason and logic together helps you break down problems, figure out causes, and find solutions.

-They Keep You Calm and Focused

When you think with reason and logic, you don't let emotions like anger or fear control your actions. You can step back and make choices that are smart, not rushed.

-Example: If someone says something hurtful, instead of snapping back, reason helps you ask, "Why are they acting this way? Is it worth arguing?"

-They Prepare You for the Future

- Logic helps you plan for what's ahead by showing you patterns and possibilities.

-Reason helps you adjust your plans when things change.

In Simple Terms:

Logic is about knowing how to think clearly, and reason is about doing it. Together, they help you navigate life smarter, solve problems faster, and make decisions that lead you toward your goals.

They're like mental tools you can use to build the future you want.

LOGICAL

The word "logical" means something that makes sense, follows clear rules, and is easy to understand because it's based on facts or reason, not emotions or guesses.

What does being logical mean?

1. Thinking clearly:

-Logical thinking is about connecting ideas in a way that makes sense step by step.

-Logical things aren't random; they follow a pattern or reason you can explain.

-Logical decisions aren't based on feelings or bias; they're based on facts.

Example of logical thinking in action:

Let's say your favorite shirt goes missing. A logical way to handle it is to:

1. Think about the last time you wore it.

2. Check your laundry or bedroom.

3. Ask if someone else has seen it.

Instead of just panicking or blaming someone without evidence.

In simple terms,

being logical means thinking in a way that's clear, reasonable, and makes sense for the situation. It's like using your brain to connect the dots and figure things out.

REASONABLE:

"Reasonable" means something that makes sense, is fair, and is based on good thinking.

When someone or something is reasonable, it's not extreme or over-the-top, but balanced and logical.

When something is reasonable, it's supported by facts, logic, or fairness.

What does being reasonable look like?

1. Using common sense

Reasonable means thinking things through and making choices that most people would agree are fair or sensible.

2. Being fair to others:

Reasonable means not expecting too much from someone or treating them unfairly.

-Example: If you're working on a group project, asking everyone to contribute equally is reasonable, but expecting someone else to do the entire thing isn't.

3. Not overreacting:

Reasonable people don't blow things out of proportion. They stay calm and handle situations in a balanced way.

In simple terms, being reasonable is about doing what makes sense for you and the people around you—it's about balance, fairness, and clear thinking.

PRACTICAL:

The word "practical" means focusing on what works in real life, not just ideas or theories.

It's about doing things in a way that's useful, realistic, and makes sense for the situation.

What does being practical look like?

1. Choosing what's realistic:

Practical decisions are things you can actually do, not just things that sound good in theory.

2. Focusing on results:

Practical means thinking about what will actually solve a problem or get things done.

- Example: If your bike chain comes off, a practical move is to fix it instead of just complaining you can't ride it.

3. Using resources wisely:

Being practical means not wasting time, energy, or money.

- Example: If you're studying for a test, it's practical to focus on the topics you don't understand rather than spending time on things you already know.

4. Being prepared for the real world:

Practical thinking helps you focus on skills or actions that are useful in your everyday life.

- Example: Learning how to budget your allowance is practical because it helps you manage money better as you grow up.

In simple terms, being practical is about doing what works and makes sense, instead of overthinking or chasing ideas that might not help you in real life. It's all about keeping it real!

REASONING:

"Reasoning" means thinking through something step by step to understand it, solve a problem, or make a decision. It's like using your brain to figure things out in a logical way. Reasoning helps you connect the dots (Based on FACTS and Evidence). It's about putting pieces of information together to come up with a conclusion.

- Example: If it's cloudy and you hear thunder, you reason that it's probably going to rain, so you grab an umbrella.

Asking "why?" and "how?":

It's about questioning things and thinking about what makes sense.

"Solving problems"

Reasoning helps you figure out what to do in tricky situations.

- Example: If your phone battery is low and you're going out, you might reason,

"I should bring my charger or use my phone less to save battery."

"Making decisions:"

When you reason, you weigh your options to pick the best one.

- Example: If you have $10, you might reason, "Should I buy snacks now, or save this for a movie ticket later?"

Types of reasoning:

- Logical reasoning:

Using facts and rules to reach a conclusion.

- Example: If all dogs bark, and Max is a dog, then Max must bark.

- Emotional reasoning:

Thinking based on feelings (which can sometimes lead to mistakes).

- Example: "I feel like I can't do this, so I shouldn't even try" (not always accurate).

In simple terms,

Reasoning is like your brain's toolbox—it helps you figure out what's going on, make sense of things, and come up with smart solutions.

RATIONAL THINKING:

Rational thinking is about using your brain to make decisions and solve problems in a way that makes sense. It's like taking a step back, looking at all the facts, and making choices based on what's logical and reasonable, not just what you feel in the moment or what someone else tells you.

Here's how it works:

Think logically:

This means connecting the dots in a way that follows a clear path.

Stay objective:

Try not to let your feelings or personal opinions take over.

For instance: if you don't like a teacher but they're giving you good advice, rational thinking means listening to the advice anyway because it's helpful.

Use evidence:

Base your choices on real facts and information, not just guesses or rumors.

For Instance:

If your friend tells you something wild, it's wise to check if it's accurate before believing it.

Ask questions:

Don't just accept what people say. Think critically and ask yourself, "Does this make sense? Is there another way to see it?"

In simple terms:

Rational thinking is about using your head instead of just going with your gut, so you can make better choices that lead to better outcomes.

LOGICAL THINKING:

"Logical thinking" is about using facts, rules, and clear steps to figure things out and make decisions. It's like a way of organizing your thoughts so that everything makes sense and leads to a solid answer or solution.

What does logical thinking look like?

Step-by-step problem-solving:

Logical thinking means breaking a problem into smaller parts and solving it one step at a time.

- Example: If your computer isn't working, you think: "Is it plugged in? Is the power button on? Is the screen connected? You check each thing logically instead of randomly guessing.

Looking for cause and effect:

Logical Thinking about figuring out how one thing leads to another.

- Example: If you don't study for a test, the logical result is that your grade might not be great. Logical thinking helps you see the connection between your actions and their consequences.

Making decisions based on facts:

Logical thinking means focusing on what's true and proven, not just on feelings or guesses.

- Example: If you're choosing between two phones, you compare their features and prices instead of just picking the one that "looks cool."

Why logical thinking is important:

-Instead of acting on impulse or emotion, you think things through and pick the best option.

-Logical thinking gives you a clear method to fix things instead of wasting time guessing.

-Logical Thinking helps you recognize when something doesn't add up, like a fake rumor or a bad deal.

-When you think logically, you trust your decisions because they're based on reason (evidence/facts), not luck.

Example of logical thinking:

Let's say you want to save money for new shoes, but you also love buying snacks after school.

Logical thinking would look like this:

1. How much do the shoes cost? (Get the facts.)

2. How much money do you have now? (Know your situation.)

3. How can you save up? (Plan: maybe cut back on snacks.)

4. How long will it take to save enough? (Figure out the timeline.)

In simple terms:

Logical thinking is about making sense of things, solving problems step by step, and making smart decisions based on facts, not just feelings or random guesses. It's like being your own detective for life's challenges!

RATIONAL & LOGICAL THINKING

What's the difference between Rational thinking and Logical thinking?

Both rational thinking and logical thinking are ways of using your brain to make good decisions, but they're a little different:

1. Logical Thinking is about following clear rules or steps to solve a problem or understand something..

"How it works"

Logical thinking is like solving a puzzle—you follow clear steps without letting emotions or other factors distract you.

2. Rational Thinking is about making decisions based on what's reasonable and realistic for the situation.

It's more flexible and considers emotions, context, and goals.

- Rational thinking helps you determine the best choice for you, not just what logically makes sense.

How it works:

Rational Thinking combines logic with emotions, goals, and real-life situations. It's less about rules and more about what's reasonable.

(It's a way of thinking that adds the equation "human characteristics and other factors of life)

Key Difference

-Rational thinking is about making smart, real-world decisions based on both logic and your personal situation.

-Logical thinking is about following strict rules of reasoning to come to a conclusion, even if it's not practical in the real world.

Think of it like this: Logical thinking solves the "how" of a problem, while rational thinking asks, "Does this make sense overall for me?"

For Personal Growth

-Logical Thinking helps you solve problems step by step, so you can handle challenges without panicking.

For example: If you're struggling with a subject at school, logical thinking helps you break it down:

"What do I not understand? Who can help me?"

- Rational Thinking helps you balance logic with emotions and long-term goals.

For instance:

If you're feeling stressed about school, rational thinking might say, "It's okay to take a break now because it'll help me focus better later."

Less Stress:

When you think logically and rationally, you avoid acting on impulse or letting emotions take over, which keeps you calm and in control.

Clear Goals:

Rational thinking helps you prioritize what really matters, while logical thinking helps you create a plan to reach those goals.

Together, they make you more confident, calm, and better at handling life.

For Financial Success

- Logical Thinking Helps you manage your money by understanding numbers and facts.

For example, if you earn $100 and want to save $40, you logically know you can spend $60 but no more.

- Rational Thinking: Helps you make financial decisions that work for your personal situation.

For example: It might be logical to save every penny, but "Rational "Thinking" considers your happiness too—so you might decide it's okay to spend some money on things you enjoy while still saving responsibly.

Avoiding Mistakes:

- Rational thinking stops you from wasting money on things you don't really need.

- Logical thinking helps you analyze deals to avoid scams or bad investments.

Building Wealth:

- Rational thinking encourages long-term planning, like saving for college or investing.

- Logical thinking helps you calculate risks and rewards to make smart financial moves.

In short,

"Rational thinking" is about making good decisions for your life, while "Logical thinking" is about solving problems with clear steps.

Together, they help you grow as a person and build a successful future.

IRRATIONAL THINKING:

What is Irrational Thinking?

- Irrational thinking is when your thoughts or decisions don't make sense because they're based on emotions, fears, or assumptions instead of facts or logic. It's like your brain is reacting to how you feel in the moment rather than thinking clearly about what's true.

Examples of Irrational Thinking:

Jumping to conclusions:

Assuming something without proof.

- Thinking the worst will happen, even if it's unlikely.
- Example: "If I fail this test, my whole life will be ruined."

(This isn't realistic—one test won't define your whole future.)

Ignoring evidence:

Refusing to see the facts because of your feelings.

- Example: "Nobody likes me," even though your friends have shown they care.

Reacting emotionally:

Letting feelings, like anger or fear, control your thoughts.

- Example: "I'll never get better at basketball, so I should quit," just because you had one bad game.

ILLOGICAL THINKING:

What is Illogical Thinking?

- Illogical thinking is when your thoughts don't follow clear or consistent reasoning.

It's like trying to solve a puzzle but putting the wrong pieces together, so your conclusions don't make sense.

Examples of Illogical Thinking:

- Making random connections:

Linking things that have nothing to do with each other.

- Example: "It rained today because I forgot my umbrella."

(Rain isn't caused by whether you have your umbrella or not.)

- Contradicting yourself:

Saying or believing two things that can't both be true.

- Example: "I want to save money, but I'm going to spend all of it on stuff I don't need."

- Skipping logical steps:

Jumping to conclusions without enough information.

- Example: "If I eat one candy, I'll gain a ton of weight."

(One candy won't have that big of an effect.)

Irrational & Illogical Thinking:

The Difference Between Irrational and Illogical Thinking

- Irrational thinking comes from emotions or assumptions, ignoring facts or reality.

- Illogical thinking comes from faulty reasoning, where your thought process doesn't make sense.

- Example: "If I wear my lucky socks, I'll ace the test."

(There's no logical connection between socks and test performance.)

Why They're Harmful

1 Irrational Thinking

- Makes you overreact or assume the worst.

- Stops you from trying new things because of unnecessary fears.

- Example: "I won't apply for the job because I'll never get it," even though you might.

2. Illogical Thinking:

- Leads to bad decisions because your reasoning doesn't add up.

- Wastes time solving problems the wrong way.

- Example: "If I skip breakfast, I'll do better on my exam."

(This isn't logical; skipping food could make you tired.)

How to Avoid Irrational and Illogical Thinking

1. Pause and reflect:

Ask yourself, "Does this make sense? Am I basing this on facts or just emotions?"

2. Challenge your thoughts:

If something sounds extreme or doesn't add up, think about why you believe it.

3. Focus on evidence:

Look for facts or logical steps to back up your ideas.

In Simple Terms

-Irrational thinking: Acting or deciding based on feelings instead of facts.

-Illogical thinking: Making conclusions that don't make sense or follow the rules of reasoning.

Both can cause problems, but learning to slow down and think critically can help you make smarter, better decisions.

IMPULSIVE:

"Impulsive" means acting quickly without thinking about the consequences. When you're impulsive, you do things in the moment because of how you feel, without stopping to ask yourself if it's a good idea.

What does being impulsive look like?

1. Acting on emotion:

You let your feelings control your actions instead of thinking things through.

- Example: You're angry, so you yell at someone or slam a door without thinking

about how it might hurt their feelings or get you in trouble.

2. Making snap decisions:

You make choices without considering the pros and cons or the possible outcomes.

3. Not planning ahead:

Being impulsive means doing what feels good or fun in the moment, even if it causes problems later.

Why is it important to understand impulsiveness?

-It can lead to mistakes:

When you act without thinking, you might do something you regret,

like saying something hurtful or spending money you don't have.

- It affects relationships:

Being impulsive can make people feel like you don't care about their feelings because

you act without considering how your actions affect them.

-It stops you from reaching goals:

Acting impulsively can distract you from your long-term plans, like saving money, studying, or improving at a skill.

How to handle being impulsive

-Pause and think:

Before acting, ask yourself, "Will I regret this later? Does this help me or hurt me?"

-Focus on your goals:

Remind yourself what's important, like saving money, doing well in school, or keeping good relationships.

-Practice self-control: Learn to say no to impulses when they don't make sense for your future.

Example of impulsive behavior:

- Your friend dares you to skip class. You impulsively say yes without thinking about the fact you'll miss important lessons and get in trouble.

Example of self-control:

- Your friend dares you to skip class, but you stop and think, "I don't want to get in trouble or fall behind in school," so you say no.

In simple terms:

Being impulsive is when you act on a whim without stopping to think about whether it's a good idea. Learning to control impulsiveness can help you make smarter decisions and avoid problems!

OBJECTIVE JUDGEMENT:

What does "objective" mean?

The word "objective" means focusing on facts instead of personal feelings, opinions, or emotions. When you're objective, you look at things fairly and logically without letting your own biases or preferences get in the way.

What is objective Judgement?

-Objective Judgement means analyzing a situation or problem by looking at the facts and evidence, instead of letting emotions or personal beliefs affect your judgment. It's like being a fair referee—you stick to what's real and ignore anything that clouds your view.

What does objective judgment look like?

1. Focusing on facts:

Objective Judgement is about looking at what's true, not just what you "feel" is true.

- Example: If you fail a test, instead of thinking "I'm just bad at math," you objectively ask, "What mistakes did I make, and how can I improve next time?"

2. Being fair: It means looking at all sides of a situation, even if you don't agree with them.

- Example: If two friends argue, you listen to both their stories before deciding who's right, instead of just siding with your favorite friend.

3. Not letting emotions control you:

It's about thinking logically, even when you feel upset or excited.

- Example: If you're angry at your teacher for giving you a bad grade, objective thinking helps you ask, "Did I do the work correctly?" instead of blaming the teacher.

Why is objective judgment good for personal growth?

1. Helps you improve:

When you're objective, you can look at your strengths and weaknesses honestly and figure out how to get better.

- Example: If you didn't make the team, you don't give up or blame others. Instead, you ask, "What skills do I need to work on?"

2. Makes better decisions:

Objective Judgement helps you make more intelligent choices by focusing on what's logical, not what you feel in the moment.

- Example: You want to stay up late watching videos, but you know objectively that getting enough sleep is better for your health and focus.

3. Keeps you calm:

When you think objectively, you're less likely to overreact or let emotions take over in tough situations.

Why is objective thinking good for financial success?

1. Avoids emotional spending:

Objective thinking helps you focus on needs vs. wants, so you don't waste money on impulse purchases.

- Example: You see cool shoes you want, but you objectively think, "Do I really need them, or should I save this money for something more important?"

2. Helps with smart planning:

You can set financial goals and stick to them by focusing on facts, like how much you need to save or spend.

- Example: If you want to buy a car, objective judgement helps you research costs and save realistically, instead of just hoping you'll somehow afford it.

3. Keeps you from being tricked:

Objective Judgement helps you look at deals, offers, or investments critically, so you don't fall for scams.

- Example: If someone promises you "easy money," you ask, "Does this actually make sense?" instead of jumping in.

In short:

- Being objective means focusing on facts and fairness.

- Objective Judgement is about using facts to make smart, balanced decisions, without letting emotions or biases take over. It's good for "Personal growth" because it helps you see the truth, improve yourself, and make better choices. It's good for "Financial success" because it helps you avoid mistakes, stick to your goals, and manage your money wisely.

SUBJECTIVE JUDGEMENT:

Subjective Judgement is when your thoughts, opinions, or decisions are influenced by your personal feelings, experiences, or preferences instead of facts or evidence. It's about how you see things based on your emotions or perspective, which might not always match reality.

What does subjective judgement look like?

1. Based on personal feelings:

Instead of focusing on facts, subjective judgement is shaped by how something makes you feel.

- Example: You think a movie is amazing because it reminded you of a fun memory, even though others might not feel the same way.

2. Influenced by bias:

It's about looking at things through your own perspective, which might not be completely fair or balanced.

- Example: You believe your best friend should win an award, even if another person objectively deserves it more.

3. Different for everyone:

Because subjective judgement depends on personal feelings, two people might have very different opinions about the same thing.

- Example: You might think broccoli tastes terrible, but someone else loves it. That's subjective.

When is subjective judgement useful?

- Expressing opinions:

It's totally fine to think subjectively when sharing how you feel about art, music, food, or anything where personal taste matters.

- Example: "I love this song because it makes me happy" is subjective, and it's valid because it's about your personal experience.

- Understanding emotions:

Subjective judgement helps you reflect on how you feel and why, which can be important for personal growth.

When can subjective thinking cause problems?

1. Ignoring facts:

If you only think subjectively, you might let emotions cloud your judgment and ignore the truth.

- Example: You believe you failed a test because the teacher doesn't like you, but the real reason is you didn't study enough.

2. Being unfair:

Subjective judgment can lead to biased decisions if you prioritize your feelings over logic or fairness.

- Example: Choosing your friend for a team project even though someone else is more qualified.

3. Making poor decisions:

Acting only on how you feel in the moment (subjective thinking) might lead to impulsive choices you regret later.

The difference between subjective and objective judgement:

- Subjective judgement: Based on personal feelings, opinions, and experiences.

- Example: "This restaurant is the best because I love the food."

- Objective judgement: Based on facts, logic, and fairness.

- Example: "This restaurant has good reviews, affordable prices, and fresh ingredients."

In simple terms:

Subjective Judgement is about seeing the world through your own feelings and opinions. While it's fine in personal situations, like deciding what you like or dislike, it's important to balance it with "Objective Judgement" when you need to make fair, fact-based decisions.

FORESIGHT & OPTIMISM:

What is Foresight?

Foresight is the ability to think ahead and predict what might happen in the future. It's about planning for what's coming and making smart decisions now to prepare for it. It's like looking ahead and preparing for challenges or opportunities before they happen.

Examples of Foresight:

1. Planning for success:

You study for a big test days ahead because you know last-minute cramming won't work.

2. Avoiding problems:

You bring an umbrella because you see clouds and think it might rain. It's about taking steps now to prepare for what's ahead.

3. Saving for the future:

You decide to save part of your money instead of spending it all, knowing you'll need it later.

4. Being proactive

Acting early to avoid problems or take advantage of opportunities. Why Foresight is Good for Personal Growth and Financial Success:

- For personal growth:

- It helps you make decisions that lead to better results in the future.

- Example: Practicing a skill regularly instead of procrastinating helps you improve faster.

- For financial success:

- Foresight helps you manage your money wisely by thinking about long-term needs, like saving for college or emergencies.

- Example: Investing in good-quality items that las instead of buying cheap ones that break quickly.

Optimism:

What is Optimism?

Optimism means having a positive attitude and expecting good things to happen, even when life is hard. It's about focusing on the bright side and believing you can handle challenges while focusing on possibilities instead of problems. It doesn't mean ignoring problems—it means focusing on solutions and believing you can overcome obstacles.

Examples of Optimism:

1. Staying motivated:

You miss making the basketball team but think, "I'll work harder and try again next year."

2. Finding solutions:

Instead of giving up when you fail a test, you believe, "I can improve if I study differently next time."

3. Seeing opportunities:

You don't get a job you wanted but think, "There's something better out there for me."

Why Optimism is Good for Personal Growth and Financial Success:

- For personal growth:

- Optimism keeps you motivated to work toward your goals, even when things don't go as planned.

- It helps you bounce back from failure because you believe things can get better.

- For financial success

- Optimism helps you stay confident in your ability to achieve financial goals, like saving money or starting a business.

- Optimism encourages you to believe in your financial goals, like starting a small business or investing, even if it takes time to succeed.

Foresight & Optimism:

How Foresight and Optimism Work Together:

- Foresight helps you plan ahead and make smart decisions now.

- Optimism keeps you positive and motivated, even if the road gets tough.

In simple terms:

-Foresight is about thinking ahead and being ready for what's next, so you're always one step ahead of life's surprises

In simple terms:

-Optimism is about having the right attitude to stay hopeful and keep going, even when things are tough.

-Optimism is about choosing to see the good in situations, staying hopeful, and believing that your actions can make things better. It's like having a mental "sunshine" that helps you keep going, no matter how cloudy life gets!

Together, they help you grow as a person, achieve your goals, and build a successful financial future.

SHORT-SIGHTEDNESS:

The opposite of "foresight" is "short-sightedness" It means focusing only on the present or immediate situation without considering the long-term consequences or future possibilities.

What Does Short-Sightedness Look Like?

1. Not planning for the future:

Ignoring how current actions might affect you later.

- Example: Spending all your money on something fun now and having nothing left when you need it later.

2. Making impulsive decisions:

Acting without thinking about long-term outcomes.

- Example: Skipping studying for a test to play video games, only to fail the test and hurt your grades.

3. Ignoring potential problems:

Not preparing for challenges that could happen down the road.

- Example: Not bringing a jacket on a cold day because it feels warm in the morning.

Why is Short-Sightedness a Problem?

- Creates avoidable mistakes:

Without thinking ahead, you might end up in situations that could have been prevented.

- Misses opportunities:

You might not take steps now that would help you succeed later.

- Causes stress:

Acting without planning often leads to last-minute problems or regrets.

In Short:

If "foresight" is looking ahead and preparing for the future, the opposite —"short-sightedness"—is focusing only on the now and ignoring how today's choices affect tomorrow. While it's okay to enjoy the moment, balancing it with foresight leads to better outcomes in life!

PESSIMISM:

"Pessimism" means having a negative attitude and expecting bad things to happen. It's like always focusing on the worst-case scenario or assuming that things won't work out, even if there's a chance they could.

What Does Pessimism Look Like?

1. Expecting failure

- Example: You think, "I'm probably going to fail this test," even though you've studied and have a good chance of doing well.

2. Focusing on the bad side of things:

- Example: If you win second place in a competition, instead of being proud, you think, "I wasn't good enough to win first."

3. Believing problems can't be solved:

- Example: If you have trouble in a subject, pessimism makes you think, "I'll never understand this," instead of trying to improve.

Why Can Pessimism Be a Problem?

1. It holds you back:

When you're pessimistic, you're less likely to try because you already believe you'll fail.

- Example: Not trying out for a team because you think, "I'll never make it anyway."

2. It adds stress:

Always expecting the worst makes you feel more anxious and unhappy.

- Example: Thinking, "Everything is going to go wrong," before a big event can make you too nervous to enjoy it.

3. It affects your relationships:

Pessimism can make it harder to connect with others because negative energy pushes people away.

How Pessimism Is Different From Being Realistic

- Pessimism:

You expect things to go wrong, even if there's no reason to think that way.

- Example: "No one will like my idea because it's probably dumb."

- Realism:

You look at the facts and make a balanced judgment.

- Example: "My idea might need some work, but people could like it if I explain it well."

How to Handle Pessimism

If you notice you're being pessimistic, try to:

- Challenge your thoughts:

Ask yourself, "Is this really true, or am I just assuming the worst?"

- Focus on solutions:

Instead of thinking about what could go wrong, focus on what you can do to make things better.

- Practice gratitude:

Think about what's going well in your life instead of only focusing on what's wrong.

In simple terms:

Pessimism is like wearing dark glasses that make everything look worse than it really is. While it's okay to be cautious sometimes, too much pessimism can stop you from trying new things, solving problems, or enjoying life.

NEGATIVITY:

Negativity is the attitude, mindset, or tendency to focus on the bad side of things, expect the worst, or emphasize problems rather than solutions. It can involve being overly critical, pessimistic, or dismissive about situations, people, or outcomes.

Key Aspects of Negativity:

1. Focusing on problems: Always seeing what's wrong instead of what's going well.
- Example: "Even though I passed the test, I only got a B, so it's not good enough."

2. Expecting the worst: Believing that bad things will happen, even when there's no reason to think so.
- Example: "I'll never get that job, so why bother applying?"

3. Being overly critical: Finding flaws in everything, even when there's no real issue.
- Example: "This party is boring," even though others are having fun.

4. Draining energy: Negativity often brings others down, as it focuses on complaints and discouragement.

Why Is Negativity Harmful?

1. Limits personal growth: If you're always focusing on the negatives, it's harder to see opportunities or learn from challenges.

2. Affects relationships: Being negative can push people away because they might feel drained or unsupported.

3. Creates stress: Constantly thinking about what's wrong can lead to anxiety or unhappiness.

While it's okay to recognize problems, being stuck in negativity can stop you from enjoying life or reaching your goals.

HATRED:

Hatred is an intense feeling of dislike, anger, or hostility toward someone or something. It goes beyond mild annoyance or frustration—it's a deep, strong emotion that can lead to negative thoughts or actions.

Key Aspects of Hatred:

1. Strong Dislike:

A powerful feeling of rejecting or opposing someone or something.

- Example: "I can't stand that person and want nothing to do with them."

2. Hostility:

Hatred often involves a sense of anger or aggression toward the object of dislike.

- Example: Feeling so upset with someone that you want to hurt them emotionally or physically.

3. Intensity:

Hatred is more extreme than disliking or being annoyed by something—it consumes more of your thoughts and feelings.

4. Can be directed toward:

- People: An individual, group, or society.

- Things or situations: Like a job, a type of music, or even a memory.

Why Is Hatred Harmful?

1. Hurts relationships:

Hatred often causes fights, broken friendships, or divisions between people.

2. Affects your well-being:

Holding onto hatred can make you feel stressed, angry, or bitter, which can harm your mental and physical health.

3. Clouds judgment:

Hatred can make it harder to think rationally or find peaceful solutions to problems.

In Simple Terms:

Hatred is a strong, negative emotion that makes you want to push something or someone away, often with anger or aggression.

While it's okay to dislike things, letting hatred take over can make life harder and prevent positive growth.

YOUR GOALS:

"Your goals" refers to the things you want to achieve in your life. These are the personal, academic, career, or life targets you set for yourself that give you something to work toward. Goals can be big or small, short-term or long-term, but they're always about what matters to "you" and what you want to accomplish.

What Are Goals?

1. Your aspirations: The dreams and achievements that are important to you.

2. Your motivation: Goals give you a reason to work hard and improve.

3. Your plans for the future: Goals help you focus on what you want your life to look like.

Why Are Goals Important?

- They give you direction: Goals help you figure out where to focus your time and energy.

- They help you grow: Working toward goals pushes you to improve and become better at things.

- They create purpose: Goals make your actions feel meaningful and rewarding.

Types of Goals

1. Short-term goals: Things you want to achieve soon.

2. Long-term goal: Bigger things that take more time and effort.

In Simple Terms:

Your goals are like a map for your life. They show you where you want to go and give you a reason to keep moving forward. Whether it's something small or life-changing, goals are about what you want and how you plan to make it happen.

YOUR DREAMS:

"Your Dreams" refers to the hopes, aspirations, and desires that inspire you and give meaning to your life. These are the things you imagine achieving or experiencing, often tied to your deepest passions and ambitions. Your dreams are personal, and they reflect what truly matters to you.

What Are Dreams?

1. Your biggest hopes: Dreams are about what you truly wish for, even if they feel far away right now.

   - Example: Becoming a famous artist, traveling the world, or making a difference in people's lives.

2. Your inspiration: Dreams fuel your imagination and keep you excited about the future.

- Example: Thinking about owning your own business motivates you to work hard today.

3. Your inner vision: Dreams are the picture you have of the life you want to live.

- Example: Seeing yourself on stage performing or building a successful career.

How Dreams Are Different from Goals

- Dreams are your big, overarching desires—the "what ifs" that inspire you.

- Example: "I dream of becoming a professional athlete."

- Goals are the steps you take to make your dreams a reality.

- Example: "I'll practice every day to improve my skills."

Why Are Dreams Important?

1. They give you purpose: Dreams help you imagine what's possible and give you something to work toward.

2. They keep you motivated: Even during tough times, dreams remind you why you're pushing forward.

- Example: "This math class is hard, but I'll stick with it because I dream of becoming an engineer."

3. They spark creativity: Dreams encourage you to think big and explore new ideas.

-Types of Dreams

1. Personal dreams: Things that make you happy or fulfilled.

- Example: Having a family, learning to play an instrument, or running a marathon.

2. Career dreams: Ambitions related to your future job or profession.

- Example: Becoming a doctor, author, or entrepreneur.

3. Impact dreams: Desires to make the world better.

- Example: Helping your community or starting a charity.

In Simple Terms:

Your dreams are the things that excite you and make life feel meaningful. They're the "what ifs" that push you to imagine a better future for yourself. While they might seem far off at times, they give you direction, hope, and a reason to keep striving for something amazing.

YOUR OBJECTIVE:

"Your Objective" refers to a specific goal or purpose you are working toward. Unlike dreams, which can be big and imaginative, or goals, which can be broad, an objective is "clear, focused, and actionable"—something you aim to achieve within a specific timeframe or with a particular result in mind.

What Are Objectives?

1. A clear target:

Objectives are precise things you want to accomplish.

- Example: "Finish this project by the end of the week" is an objective.

2. A step toward a larger goal:

Objectives are smaller, specific parts of a bigger plan.

- Example: If your goal is to get into college, an objective might be to improve your math grade this semester.

3. Action-oriented:

Objectives focus on what you need to do, not just what you hope for.

- Example: "Save $50 this month" is an objective, while "I want to be rich" is a dream.

Why Are Objectives Important?

1. They give direction:

Objectives help you stay focused by defining precisely what needs to be done.

- Example: If your objective is to pass a test, you'll know you need to study specific chapters.

2. They make progress measurable:

You can track your success with objectives because they're specific.

- Example: "Lose 5 pounds in 2 months" is an objective you can measure.

3. They help you prioritize:

Objectives make it easier to decide what's most important to work on right now.

- Example: "Complete my college application this week" helps you focus on the task at hand.

How Objectives Fit with Dreams and Goals

- Dreams: The big picture of what you want in life.

- Example: "I want to travel the world."

- Goals: Broader plans to achieve your dreams.

- Example: "Save money for travel."

- Objectives: Specific actions that bring you closer to your goals and dreams.

- Example: "Save $100 every month for the next year."

In Simple Terms:

Your objective is your "immediate target"—the specific thing you're working to accomplish right now. It's focused, actionable, and helps you make steady progress toward your bigger goals and dreams.

YOUR PURPOSE:

"Your purpose" refers to the reason behind what you do or what drives you in life. It's the deeper meaning or motivation that gives your actions direction and makes your life feel meaningful. Your purpose is about understanding "why" you're working toward something, not just what you're doing.

What Is "Your Purpose"?

1. Your "why":

It's the reason behind your goals and dreams—the thing that inspires you to keep going.

- Example: "I want to help people feel better" might be your purpose if you dream of becoming a doctor.

2. Your guiding force:

It's what helps you make decisions and figure out what's important.

- Example: If your purpose is to create a better future, you might focus on education or helping your community.

3. A source of fulfillment:

Living with purpose makes your life feel meaningful because you're working toward something that truly matters to you.

- Example: "My purpose is to make the world a kinder place" gives you a reason to act kindly every day.

How Purpose Is Different from Goals and Objectives

- Purpose is your reason or motivation—the "why."

- Example: "I want to make a difference in the world."

- Goals are what you're working toward—the "what."

- Example: "I want to become a teacher."

- Objectives are the specific actions to reach your goals—the "how."

- Example: "I'll take a teaching certification course this year."

Why Is Knowing Your Purpose Important?

1. It keeps you motivated:

When you know why something matters, it's easier to stay committed.

- Example: If your purpose is to help others, you'll work hard in school to gain the skills you need to do that.

2. It helps you make decisions:

Your purpose acts as a guide for choosing what's important.

- Example: If your purpose is to protect the environment, you might choose to study environmental science or volunteer for clean-up efforts.

3. It brings you happiness:

Working toward something meaningful makes life more fulfilling.

- Example: If your purpose is to inspire others, you'll find joy in small moments where you make someone's day better.

In Simple Terms

Your purpose is the "reason behind everything you do". It's the deeper "why" that inspires your goals, dreams, and actions. When you know your purpose, it helps you stay focused, make better choices, and live a more meaningful life.

YOUR PRIORITIES:

"Your priorities" refers to the things in your life that are most important to you and deserve your focus, time, and energy. These are the tasks, goals, or values you choose to put first because they matter the most to your happiness, success, or well-being.

What Are Priorities?

1. What matters most to you:

Your priorities reflect what's important in your life.

- Example: Spending time with family, getting good grades, or improving your health.

2. What you focus on first:

They help you decide what to do before anything else.

- Example: If studying for a test is your priority, you'll do that before hanging out with friends.

3. How you manage your time:

Priorities guide how you divide your time and energy.

- Example: If your goal is to save money, your priority might be sticking to a budget instead of spending on entertainment.

Why Are Priorities Important?

1. They keep you focused:

When you know what matters most, you're less likely to waste time on things that don't help you.

- Example: If your priority is improving at basketball, you'll spend more time practicing and less time on distractions.

2. They help you make decisions:

Priorities make it easier to choose what's worth your time.

- Example: If your priority is preparing for college, you might decide to take advanced classes instead of skipping them for easier options.

3. They balance your life:

By setting priorities, you can focus on what's important without feeling overwhelmed.

- Example: You might prioritize school during the week and friends or hobbies on weekends.

Types of Priorities

1. Short-term priorities: Things you need to focus on right now.

- Example: Completing a project that's due tomorrow.

2. Long-term priorities: Things that matter to your future.

- Example: Saving for college or building a skill for your dream career.

3. Personal priorities: Things that are important for your happiness and well-being.

- Example: Taking care of your mental health or spending time with loved ones.

In Simple Terms:

Your priorities are the things that matter most to you right now and in the future. They help you focus your time and energy on what's truly important so you can stay on track and live a more meaningful life. Knowing your priorities makes it easier to achieve your goals and remain balanced.

STAY FOCUSED:

"Stay focused" means keeping your attention on what's important and avoiding distractions. It's about staying on track with your goals or tasks so you can finish them successfully without letting other things pull you away.

What Does It Mean to Stay Focused?

1. Concentrating on one thing at a time:

It's about putting all your energy into the task you're working on.

- Example: If you're studying for a test, staying focused means ignoring your phone or TV until you're done.

2. Avoiding distractions:

Staying focused means not letting things that don't matter get in the way.

- Example: If your goal is to finish a school project, staying focused means you will resist the urge to scroll through social media.

3. Keeping your goal in mind:

Staying focused helps you remember why you're doing something and work steadily toward it.

- Example: If your dream is to improve in basketball, staying focused means practicing regularly, even when it feels hard.

Why Is Staying Focused Important?

1. You finish things faster:

When you stay focused, you get your work done more efficiently.

- Example: Finishing your homework quickly so you have free time later.

2. You achieve better results:

Concentrating fully helps you do your best work.

- Example: Writing a great essay because you weren't distracted while writing it.

3. You reach your goals:

Staying focused keeps you on track toward what you want to achieve.

- Example: Saving money for something important instead of spending it on random things.

How to Stay Focused

1. Set clear goals:

Know exactly what you're trying to accomplish.

- Example: "I will study math for 30 minutes without distractions."

2. Remove distractions:

Turn off your phone, find a quiet space, or use tools like timers to help you stay on task.

- Example: Using a timer to focus for 25 minutes before taking a short break.

3. Take breaks when needed:

Short breaks can help you stay fresh and keep your focus longer.

- Example: Stretching or walking for five minutes after an hour of focused work.

In Simple Terms:

"Stay focused" means giving your full attention to what matters and not letting distractions get in the way. It's like putting on blinders to keep your eyes on your goals, so you can get things done and achieve success faster.

Pt. 4 Chapter 2 Characteristics

Belief:

Belief is the mindset of accepting and trusting that you have the ability, potential, and tools to grow and achieve success. It's the confidence that the effort you put into something will lead to improvement and results over time.

Belief in growth and success is like saying, "I know I can get better if I keep trying." It's trusting that progress is possible, even if things feel hard right now. This belief keeps you motivated to stick with the process, no matter how slow or challenging it might seem.

For example:

- When you study for a big test, belief is what helps you think, "If I put in the work, I'll do well."

- If you're learning a new skill, like playing guitar or coding, belief is what tells you, *"I might not be great today, but if I keep practicing, I'll get there."*

Belief in the process is about focusing on the small steps and trusting they'll add up to something big. It's not about having everything figured out right away; it's about knowing that improvement takes time and effort—and being okay with that.

Without belief, you might give up too soon. With belief, you keep pushing forward because you trust that growth and success are possible if you stay committed.

Action:

Taking action means actively doing something to move closer to your goals. It's the step-by-step effort that turns your ideas, dreams, or plans into actual progress and results.

Taking action is like stepping onto the path to get where you want to go. It's not just thinking about your goals or dreaming about success—it's doing the work to make it happen.

Even small actions matter. They're like bricks that you lay one by one to build something big.

You don't have to have everything figured out to start—you just need to take that first step. Over time, all those small steps add up to real progress.

Without action, nothing changes. But when you take action, you learn, grow, and get

closer to success, even if things don't work out perfectly every time. Taking action is how you turn belief into reality.

Faith:

Faith is the trust and confidence that the efforts you put in now will lead to positive results, even if you don't see immediate success. It's believing in the journey, the process, and your potential to grow and succeed over time.

Faith in growth and success is like planting a seed.

You can't see the tree yet, but you believe that if you water it, give it sunlight, and take care of it, it will grow into something amazing. You trust that all your hard work and patience will pay off, even if it takes time.

When it comes to personal growth or achieving success, having faith means believing:

- That you "can" improve, even if you're struggling right now.

- That failure isn't the end but a stepping stone to learning and getting better.

- That the effort you put into studying, practicing, or working will eventually lead to the results you want.

Faith is what keeps you going on tough days when it feels like progress is slow. It's trusting that the process—your hard work, discipline, and learning—will lead to success, even if you can't see the results yet.

Faith in the process gives you hope and motivation to keep moving forward, no matter how long it takes.

Integrity:

Integrity means being honest and doing the right thing, even when no one is watching. It's about staying true to your values and sticking to what you know is right, no matter the situation.

Integrity is like having a moral compass inside you that guides your choices. It's about being the kind of person who keeps their word, treats others with respect, and doesn't cheat or lie, even when it might be easier or more tempting to do so.

Integrity is vital because it shows people they can trust you, and it helps you respect yourself. It's not always the easiest path, but it's the one that builds your character and earns you respect. When you live with integrity, your actions match your words, and people know they can count on you to do the right thing.

Resiliency:

Resiliency is the ability to bounce back and recover from challenges, setbacks, tough situations, difficulties, or failures. It's the inner strength to keep going, adapt, and grow, even when things don't go as planned.

Resiliency is like being a rubber band—no matter how much life stretches or twists you, you find a way to snap back into shape. It's not about avoiding hard times; it's about staying strong and learning from them so you can keep moving forward.

Being resilient doesn't mean you won't feel upset, frustrated, or discouraged sometimes. It just means you don't let those feelings stop you. Instead, you find ways to adapt, solve problems, and keep believing in yourself. Resiliency helps you grow stronger and more confident every time you face a challenging situation.

Accountability:

Accountability means taking responsibility for your actions, decisions, and their outcomes. It's about owning up to what you do—both the good and the bad—and being willing to face the consequences or make things right.

Accountability is like saying, "I'm in charge of my choices, and I'll stand by them." It means you don't blame others when something goes wrong, and you're honest about your part in things. At the same time, when you succeed, you can be proud because you know it's your effort that made it happen.

Accountability shows maturity and builds trust. People respect you when you take responsibility for your actions because it shows you're honest and dependable. It's also essential for personal growth—when you hold yourself accountable, you learn from mistakes and keep improving.

Ambition:

Ambition is the strong desire to achieve something important or succeed at a goal. It's the drive that pushes you to work hard and aim for something bigger than where you are now.

Ambition is like the fire inside you that makes you want to do more, be better, or reach a dream. It's what gets you excited about your future and motivates you to put in the effort to make it happen.

Ambition doesn't mean you'll succeed instantly, but it keeps you aiming higher and working toward your goals, even when challenges come up. It's like having a vision for your future and being determined to make it real. Ambition is powerful because it helps you grow, take risks, and achieve things you didn't think were possible.

Devotion:

Devotion is deep love, loyalty, or dedication to something or someone. It means committing your time, energy, and heart to what you care about most.

Devotion is like saying, "This really matters to me, and I'll give it my all." It's about being fully committed to something you value, whether it's a person, a goal, or even a belief.

Devotion is powerful because it gives you focus and purpose. It's not just about saying you care—it's about showing it through your actions and commitment.

Being devoted means sticking with something, even when it's challenging, because it's important to you.

Consistency:

Consistency means doing something regularly and in the same way over time. It's about sticking to your habits, actions, or goals, even when it's not easy.

Consistency is like showing up every day for something that matters to you. It's not about being perfect but about staying steady and reliable in your efforts. Imagine you're learning a new skill, like playing the guitar or improving at basketball—if you practice a little bit every day, you'll get better over time. That's consistency.

Consistency is important because it creates momentum. Small actions repeated over time lead to big results. Even if progress feels slow, sticking with it helps you grow and achieve your goals. It's about being disciplined enough to keep going, even when you don't feel like it.

Perseverance:

Perseverance (consistency in the face of challenges) means not giving up, even when things get complicated. It's the determination to keep working toward your goals, no matter the challenges or setbacks.

Perseverance is like running a race where the finish line feels really far away, but you keep going anyway because you know it's worth it. It's about pushing through tough times and not letting obstacles stop you from reaching your goals.

Perseverance shows strength and determination. It's what helps you grow through challenges and proves that you can handle tough situations. Even when progress feels slow or you face setbacks, perseverance keeps you moving forward until you succeed.

Determination:

Determination is the strong decision and focus to achieve a goal, no matter what challenges come your way. It's the mindset of not letting anything stop you from reaching what you want.

Determination is like having a laser focus on something you really care about and refusing to give up, even when it gets hard. It's that inner drive that says, "I'm going to make this happen no matter what."

Determination is what pushes you to keep going, even when things feel overwhelming or you fail at first.

It's the attitude that says, "This is worth it, and I won't stop until I get there." It's a key part of success because it helps you stay focused and overcome obstacles.

Dedication:

Dedication means committing yourself fully to something important to you. It's about giving your time, energy, and focus to achieve a goal or support something you care about.

Dedication is like saying, "This matters to me, and I'm going to give it my all." It's when you stay focused and work hard at something, even when it's difficult or takes a lot of time.

Dedication shows how serious and committed you are to your goals or responsibilities.

It's about not just wanting something but being willing to put in the consistent effort to make it happen.

When you're dedicated, you don't give up easily—you keep going because it's important to you.

Discipline:

Discipline is the ability to control your actions, stick to your goals, and do what's

necessary, even when it's hard or you don't feel like it. It's about making choices that help you stay focused and consistent.

Discipline is like being your own coach. It's about telling yourself, "I need to do this, even if I'd rather do something else right now." It's not always fun, but it helps you achieve your goals and build good habits.

Discipline is like a muscle—you get stronger at it the more you use it. It helps you stay on track, overcome distractions, and push through challenging moments.

While motivation gets you started, discipline is what keeps you going when motivation fades. It's a key ingredient for success in anything you do.

Humility:

Humility is the quality of being humble, which means not thinking you're better than others. It's about recognizing your strengths and achievements without bragging and being open to learning and improving.

Humility is like being confident in yourself but not acting like you're above everyone else. It's knowing you're good at something but not needing to show off. It also means understanding that you don't have all the answers and being willing to listen and grow.

For example:

- If you're really good at something, like math or sports, humility is using your skills to help others instead of just showing off.

- If someone gives you advice or criticism, humility is being open to it instead of acting like you already know everything.

Humility doesn't mean putting yourself down or ignoring your talents. It's about being grounded, respectful, and willing to acknowledge that everyone has something valuable to contribute. When you're humble, people respect you because you respect them, too.

Gratitude:

Gratitude is the feeling of being thankful and appreciating the good things in your life, no matter how big or small they are.

Gratitude is like taking a moment to say, "Wow, I'm lucky to have this." It's about recognizing the people, opportunities, and experiences that make your life better and feeling thankful for them.

Gratitude is important because it helps you focus on the positives in life instead of constantly worrying about what's missing or what's going wrong.

It can make you feel happier and strengthen your relationships with others. Being grateful isn't just about saying "thanks"—it's about feeling it and showing it through your actions.

Pt. 4 Chapter 3
The Foundation

Prospering vs Succeeding:

The difference between prospering and succeeding lies in their scope, depth, and sustainability. While both involve achievement, prospering often implies a broader, more holistic, and enduring state of well-being, whereas succeeding is typically more specific and goal-oriented.

Aspect	Prospering	Succeeding
Definition	A state of flourishing, growth, and overall well-being in multiple aspects of life.	The accomplishment of a specific goal or objective.
Scope	Holistic, encompassing financial, emotional, relational, and spiritual dimensions.	Narrower, focusing on achieving a particular milestone or result.
Sustainability	Long-term and enduring, reflecting ongoing growth and fulfillment.	May be temporary or tied to a single achievement.
Measure of Success	Based on balance, fulfillment, and overall thriving in life.	Measured by the completion or attainment of a defined goal.
Emphasis	Focuses on living abundantly and cultivating a meaningful, flourishing life.	Focuses on achieving targets, whether personal, professional, or material.
Emotional Impact	Brings a sense of deep contentment and alignment with one's values and purpose.	Brings satisfaction or pride in accomplishing a task or overcoming a challenge.
Examples	Building a happy, thriving family; enjoying financial security with peace of mind; leaving a positive legacy.	Getting a promotion, winning a competition, or completing a project.

How They Relate:

*Succeeding as a Step Toward Prospering:

Successes can contribute to prosperity, but prosperity often requires a series of successes in various areas of life.

*Prospering Goes Beyond Succeeding:

Prosperity is not just about achieving goals but also about sustaining well-being, growth, and fulfillment over time.

Succeeding is like chasing quick wins, while prospering is like building lasting wealth.

*Succeeding (Short-Term Thinking, Weak Foundation)

Gaining quick success without integrity or solid principles, often leading to eventual collapse.

- Example: A company that cuts corners to maximize short-term profits but faces lawsuits and bankruptcy due to unethical practices.

*Prospering (Long-Term Thinking, Strong Foundation)

Growing sustainably with integrity, discipline, and honorable principles, leading to lasting success.

- Example: A farmer who nurtures the soil, rotates crops, and invests in long-term growth, ensuring a thriving farm for generations.

Succeeding can be momentary victories. It can support the belief of thinking that you're getting ahead.

Prospering is holistic. It lays the foundation that's required to get ahead and remain ahead. <u>It's about building a foundation where success keeps multiplying</u>.

In essence, succeeding is about what you achieve,

while prospering is about how you live and thrive after those achievements.

Prosperity:

Prosperity is a state of flourishing, success, and well-being that encompasses material wealth, emotional fulfillment, and a meaningful life. It is often associated with abundance, but true prosperity extends beyond financial riches to include health, relationships, personal growth, and contributions to society.

Long-Term Thinking:

The term "long-term" refers to a mindset, strategy, or approach that prioritizes achieving sustainable success, growth, or stability over an extended period rather than seeking immediate or short-term results.

When applied to building a prosperous foundation, "long-term" involves planning, investing, and making decisions that will yield lasting benefits, even if they require patience, consistent effort, and delayed gratification.

By adopting a long-term perspective, you shift your focus from immediate gratification to sustainable prosperity, ensuring financial stability and success for years to come.

Long-term thinking in the context of building a morally prosperous and successful foundation refers to adopting a mindset and approach that prioritizes ethical actions, sustainable practices, and meaningful goals to create lasting success that aligns with moral values.

*It Provides Sustainable Success:

Built on Trust, integrity, and fairness, ensuring it can withstand challenges.

*It Yields an Inner Fulfillment:

A sense of peace and alignment with one's values.

*It Builds Stronger Relationships:

Built on respect, Trust, and mutual benefit.

*It Births or Continues a Positive Legacy:

A lasting impact that benefits future generations and inspires others.

*It Renders Broader Influence:

Becoming a role model or catalyst for positive change in society. This approach ensures that your foundation is not only successful but also deeply meaningful, enriching your life and the lives of others while upholding your moral principles.

Integrity:

Integrity, in the context of building a prosperous foundation, refers to sticking to a set of righteous and honorable principles that guide decisions, actions, and relationships. It involves honesty, transparency, and consistency in your behavior, ensuring that your foundation is built on Trust, respect, and accountability. Integrity is the cornerstone of a foundation that is not only prosperous but also enduring and respected by others.

The Role of Integrity in a Prosperous Foundation:

*Trust and Reputation:

Integrity fosters trust, which is essential for building strong relationships and credibility.

*Sustainability:

Prosperity built on integrity is more likely to endure because it rests on solid ethical principles.

*Inner Fulfillment:

Acting with integrity brings peace of mind and a sense of alignment with one's values.

*Influence and Leadership:

Integrity inspires others, creating a positive ripple effect in teams, organizations, or communities.

By incorporating integrity into your foundation, you ensure that your success is not only prosperous but also meaningful, respected, and capable of withstanding the test of time.

Honorable Principles:

Honorable principles refer to a set of ethical, moral, and virtuous/righteous guidelines that serve as a compass for actions, decisions, and relationships when building a prosperous foundation. These principles prioritize fairness, respect, and the greater good, ensuring that prosperity is achieved in a way that upholds dignity, integrity, and the well-being of all involved.

Role of Honorable Principles in a Prosperous Foundation:

*Trust Building:

Honorable principles foster Trust, which is crucial for sustainable success in relationships, businesses, or communities.

*Sustainable Growth:

Prosperity grounded in honorable actions ensures that success is ethical, enduring, and mutually beneficial.

*Legacy Creation:

A foundation built on honorable principles leaves a lasting positive impact, inspiring others to uphold similar values.

*Inner Fulfillment:

Acting in alignment with honorable principles provides a sense of peace, purpose, and pride in one's achievements.

By embedding honorable principles into the foundation, you ensure that prosperity is not only achieved but also deeply meaningful, respected, and capable of making a positive and lasting difference in the world.

Upright Morals:

Upright morals refer to a strong commitment to ethical and virtuous/righteous behavior based on principles of honesty, justice, and goodness.

In the context of building a prosperous foundation, upright morals guide decisions and actions to ensure success is achieved in a way that is not only materially rewarding but also ethically sound, sustainable, and beneficial to oneself and others.

Role of Upright Morals in Building a Prosperous Foundation:

*Trust and Credibility:

Upholding upright morals fosters Trust and respect from others, creating strong relationships and networks.

*Sustainable Success:

Prosperity achieved through moral actions is more likely to endure as it is built on ethical and stable foundations.

*Positive Influence:

Acting morally inspires others, creating a ripple effect of integrity and goodness in communities or organizations.

*Inner Fulfillment:

Upright morals bring peace of mind and a sense of alignment with higher values, making success more meaningful.

*Legacy Building:

A foundation built on moral principles leaves a positive impact, benefiting future generations and setting a high standard for others to follow.

By prioritizing upright morals, you ensure that your foundation is not only prosperous but also ethically sound/good, respected, and capable of enriching lives far beyond your own.

Humility:

Humility in the context of building a prosperous foundation refers to having a balanced sense of self-awareness, where one recognizes one's strengths and achievements without arrogance while also acknowledging limitations, learning from others, and remaining open to growth. It involves valuing collaboration, respecting diverse perspectives, and prioritizing service over ego, ensuring that prosperity is achieved in a sustainable, ethical, and meaningful way.

The Role of Humility in a Prosperous Foundation:

*Fostering Collaboration:

Humility encourages teamwork and builds Trust, enabling stronger relationships and partnerships.

*Sustainable Leadership:

Humble leaders inspire loyalty and respect, creating environments where others feel valued and motivated.

*Encouraging Growth:

Humility keeps individuals open to learning and improvement, ensuring continuous development.

*Building Legacy:

A humble approach creates a lasting impact rooted in service, respect, and genuine contribution to others' well-being.

*Inner Fulfillment:

Humility brings peace and satisfaction by aligning success with values of gratitude, service, and purpose.

By practicing humility, you build a foundation that not only leads to prosperity but also creates meaningful relationships, inspires others, and leaves a positive legacy that endures far beyond your personal achievements.

Wisdom:

Wisdom is the ability to apply knowledge, experience, insight, and good judgment to make sound decisions and navigate life effectively. It goes beyond intelligence or knowledge, encompassing/surrounding an understanding of deeper truths, ethical principles, and the interconnectedness of actions and outcomes.

Wisdom often involves a balance of intellect, compassion, and intuition.

How Wisdom Differs From Knowledge:

-Knowledge is the accumulation of information and facts.

-Wisdom is the application of that knowledge in practical, meaningful, and ethical ways.

-Knowledge is "knowing that a tomato is a fruit;" Wisdom is "knowing not to put it in a fruit salad."

(because a tomato is not the same type of fruit as an apple, orange, pineapple, and other sweet fruits)

Sources of obtaining Wisdom:

*Life Experience:

Learning through personal trials, successes, and relationships.

*Reflection:

Taking time to think deeply about experiences, decisions, and their outcomes.

*Observation:

Gaining insight from observing others' lives, behaviors, and decisions.

*Learning from Others:

Seeking advice, reading, or listening to mentors, elders, or spiritual guides.

*Spiritual or Philosophical Practices:

Engaging in meditation, prayer, or contemplation to develop inner clarity and understanding.

Wisdom is the art of living well.

It is not just about knowing what to do but understanding why and how to do it in a way that promotes harmony, growth, and well-being for oneself and others.

Wisdom is Like Learning from Experience

Think of times when you've made mistakes or learned something important. Maybe you trusted someone who wasn't honest, or you tried a shortcut on homework, and it didn't work out. Wisdom is taking those lessons and using them to make better choices next time.

It's also watching others mess up or succeed and thinking, "What can I learn from that?"

Wisdom Takes Time

You don't get Wisdom all at once. It comes from trying, failing, learning, and growing. It's like leveling up in a game after beating challenges.

"Knowledge" is knowing "What To Do!"

"Wisdom" is knowing "When To Do It and When Not To Do It!"

The cool thing is that you keep getting wiser as you live and learn!

Applied Knowledge:

Applied knowledge is when you take what you've learned (knowledge) and actually use it in real-life situations.

It's the difference between just "knowing" something and "doing" something with that knowledge. It's what turns information into action, making it practical and useful.

- Examples of Applied Knowledge:

1. School and Studying:

*Knowledge: Learning math formulas in class.

*Applied Knowledge: Using those formulas to solve real-world problems, like calculating how much paint you need for a wall or budgeting your allowance.

2. Skills and Hobbies:

*Knowledge: Knowing how to read music or understanding the rules of a sport.

*Applied Knowledge: Playing a song on the piano or performing well on the field during a game.

3. Life Lessons:

*Knowledge: Knowing that procrastinating can lead to stress.

*Applied Knowledge: Planning your time wisely so you finish assignments before the deadline.

4. Work and Career:

*Knowledge: Learning how to use a new software program at work.

*Applied Knowledge: Actually using that software to complete a task or solve a problem in your job.

-Why Applied Knowledge Matters:

*Makes Learning Useful:

Knowing facts is excellent, but unless you apply them, they're just stuck in your head.

*Builds Confidence:

Using what you know helps you gain skills and feel more capable.

*Solves Problems:

Applied knowledge is how you fix things, achieve goals, and adapt to challenges.

*Leads to Growth:

When you practice using your knowledge, you learn more and get better over time.

-How to Turn Knowledge Into Applied Knowledge:

1. Practice:

Repeatedly use what you've learned in real situations.

2. Experiment:

Try different ways to apply what you know to see what works best.

3. Reflect:

Think about what you did, how it worked, and how you can improve.

4. Seek Feedback:

Ask others for input to refine your skills.

In short, "applied knowledge" is taking what's in your head and putting it into action in a way that makes a difference.

It's how you go from being informed to being capable!

Righteousness:

Righteousness is the quality of being morally right, just, and virtuous. It involves living according to principles of truth, fairness, and integrity and striving to do what is ethically and morally good.

Righteousness often goes beyond simply following rules; it reflects a deep commitment to living in alignment with higher values, whether spiritual, personal, or societal.

The Balance of Righteousness:

While righteousness is a virtue, it is important to avoid self-righteousness,

which can lead to arrogance or judgment of others.

True righteousness is marked by humility, compassion, and a willingness to forgive and grow.

In essence, righteousness is about living a life that reflects integrity, fairness, and a

commitment to what is good, creating a foundation for personal and societal harmony.

Respectfulness:

Respectfulness is the act of showing consideration, appreciation, and regard for others' feelings, rights, beliefs, and boundaries.

It reflects a sense of civility, kindness, and understanding in interactions, fostering positive relationships and mutual Trust.

Respectfulness is a cornerstone of strong, healthy communities and relationships because it values the dignity and worth of every individual.

Respectfulness means treating people the way you want to be treated.

It's about being kind, fair, and understanding toward others, no matter who they are.

Accountability:

Accountability means taking responsibility for your actions, decisions, and their consequences—whether good or bad. It's about owning up to what you do, being reliable, and following through on commitments. Being accountable shows maturity builds Trust, and helps you grow as a person.

-Why Accountability Matters:

*Builds Trust:

When people know you take responsibility for your actions, they're more likely to trust you.

*Earns Respect:

Accountability shows that you're reliable and mature.

*Helps You Grow:

Owning up to your mistakes teaches you how to improve and handle challenges better in the future.

*Creates Better Relationships:

Accountability keeps friendships and family relationships strong because people know they can depend on you.

-How to Be Accountable:

*Keep Your Promises:

Only commit to things you can actually do and follow through on them.

*Admit Mistakes:

If you mess up, don't try to cover it up. Say, "I was wrong," and work on fixing it.

*Be Honest:

Don't shift blame onto others or make excuses—be honest about what happened.

*Reflect and Learn:

Ask yourself what you can do better next time to avoid the same mistake.

*Follow Up:

If you promise to fix something, make sure you actually do it.

Quick Example:

Imagine you're supposed to mow the lawn at home, but you forget. Instead of saying,

"I didn't have time" (when you were actually on your phone), you admit, "I forgot. I'll do it now."

That's accountability—you take ownership of the mistake and take action to make it right.

In short, accountability is about being honest with yourself and others, owning your actions, and showing that you're someone people can count on. It's a skill that helps you succeed in school, relationships, and life!

Success:

Success is the accomplishment of a goal or the attainment of an objective that is meaningful to the individual or group pursuing it. It

is a measure of progress or achievement, often reflecting hard work, determination, and purpose.

Success can be personal, professional, relational, or societal, and its definition varies depending on individual values, aspirations, and perspectives.

Success is about achieving what you set out to do

Short-Term Thinking:

Short-term thinking is focusing on immediate needs, desires, or results without considering the long-term consequences of your actions. It prioritizes quick wins, instant gratification, or solving problems for the moment, often at the expense of future stability, growth, or well-being.

-Why People Fall Into Short-Term Thinking:

1. Immediate Rewards:

It feels good to get something now instead of waiting.

2. Avoiding Discomfort:

It's easier to choose what's comfortable at the moment than to face hard work or tough decisions.

3. Pressure:

Stress or time constraints can push people to focus only on solving the problem right in front of them.

4. Lack of Planning:

Without a bigger goal or plan, it's hard to think beyond today.

-Downsides of Short-Term Thinking:

1. Missed Opportunities:

You might make decisions that feel good now but limit your options later.

2. Unintended Consequences:

Short-term fixes can lead to bigger problems later.

3. Stalled Growth:

Always focusing on the present keeps you from planning for bigger goals.

-Balancing Short-Term and Long-Term Thinking:

Short-term thinking isn't always bad. Sometimes, you need to focus on the moment, like calming a friend down during an argument or finishing a last-minute project. The key is to balance short-term actions with long-term goals.

-How to Avoid Getting Stuck in Short-Term Thinking:

1. Think Ahead:

Ask yourself, "How will this choice affect me next week, next year, or in five years?"

2. Set Goals:

Know what you want in the future so you can make decisions that move you toward it.

3. Be Patient:

Remember that some of the best rewards take time and effort.

4. Learn From Mistakes:

If short-term thinking gets you into trouble, reflect on what you could do differently next time.

In summary, Short-term thinking focuses on "right now," but it's important to step back and think about how today's decisions shape your future. Balancing short-term and long-term thinking helps you make smarter choices that lead to lasting success.

Deceit:

Deceit is the act of intentionally misleading or lying to someone to gain an advantage, avoid responsibility, or achieve a personal goal. It involves dishonesty and manipulation, often at the expense of Trust and integrity in relationships or situations. Deceit can take many forms, such as outright lies, hiding the truth, or exaggerating facts to create a false impression.

In summary, deceit is about misleading others for personal benefit, but it often leads to harm, mistrust, and regret. Being truthful and taking responsibility helps you build stronger, more authentic relationships and a reputation for integrity.

The Get-Over:

A "Get-Over" type of person is someone who prioritizes their own benefit, often at the expense of others, by using manipulation, deceit, or opportunism. They focus on short-term gains and are willing to bend or break the rules, exploit situations, or take advantage of people to achieve their goals. This behavior often reflects a lack of integrity and a willingness to put self-interest above fairness or ethical considerations.

Characteristics of a "Get-Over" Type of Person:

1. Manipulative:

They use charm, lies, or persuasion to influence others for personal gain.

2. Opportunistic:

They exploit situations or people whenever they see a chance to gain something, regardless of the impact on others.

Example: Taking credit for someone else's idea or work.

3. Self-Centered:

Their focus is primarily on their own success or comfort, with little regard for fairness or others' feelings.

Example: Taking more than their fair share in group efforts or rewards.

4. Deceptive:

They frequently lie or omit the truth to avoid responsibility or gain an advantage.

Example: Pretending to know less to avoid blame or more to gain respect they haven't earned.

5. Short-Term Thinker:

They prioritize immediate rewards without considering long-term consequences for themselves or others.

Example: Borrowing money with no intention of repaying it.

6. Unreliable:

They rarely follow through on promises or commitments unless it benefits them directly.

Example: Saying they'll help with a task but disappearing when it's time to act.

7. Exploitative:

They take advantage of others' kindness, Trust, or vulnerabilities.

Example: Borrowing favors without reciprocating or exaggerating their needs to gain sympathy.

8. Blame-Shifting:

When things go wrong, they avoid accountability by shifting blame to others.

Example: Claiming someone else misunderstood their intentions when caught in a lie.

- How They Operate:

*In Friendships:

They may only stay connected as long as they can get something out of the relationship, like favors, money, or social status.

*At Work:

They might cut corners, take credit for others' work, or avoid responsibilities to climb the ladder.

*In Relationships:

They often manipulate emotions or situations to keep control or avoid contributing equally.

Consequences of Being a "Get-Over" Type of Person:

1. Loss of Trust:

People eventually recognize their behavior and stop trusting them.

2. Damaged Relationships:

Their selfish actions often lead to broken friendships or strained family bonds.

3. Reputation Issues:

Once labeled as someone who takes advantage of others, their social and professional credibility can suffer.

4. Long-Term Isolation:

Their focus on short-term gains often leaves them without meaningful connections or support.

-How to Spot a "Get-Over" Type of Person:

1. They consistently take more than they give.

2. Their stories or promises often don't match their actions.

3. They frequently justify unethical behavior as "necessary" or "no big deal."

4. They avoid accountability when caught in manipulative or exploitative behavior.

In essence, a "get-over" type of person prioritizes their self-interest at all costs, often sacrificing Trust, fairness, and integrity for personal gain. Recognizing and addressing this behavior can help protect yourself from being taken advantage of while encouraging accountability in others.

Corruption:

Corruption is the abuse of power, authority, or resources for personal gain, often at the expense of others or ethical standards. It involves dishonest or unethical behavior by individuals in positions of Trust or influence, such as government officials, business leaders, or even everyday people, and undermines fairness, justice, and the common good.

Corruption undermines Trust, fairness, and progress in society.

It reflects dishonesty and selfishness and harms everyone except those who profit from it. Combating corruption requires accountability, transparency, and a commitment to integrity at every level of society.

Disloyalty:

Disloyalty is the act of betraying Trust, failing to remain faithful, or not honoring commitments or relationships. It involves a lack of support, commitment, or faithfulness toward someone or something that deserves loyalty, such as a friend, family member, organization, or cause. Disloyalty can damage Trust, weaken bonds, and create feelings of betrayal or hurt.

In summary, disloyalty is the failure to remain faithful to trust, relationships, or commitments. It causes harm to connections and reputations, but it can be avoided by acting with honesty, empathy, and integrity.

Betrayal:

Betrayal is the act of breaking Trust or faith in someone by going against their expectations, confidence, or loyalty. It often involves deception, dishonesty, or actions that harm someone who trusted or depended on you. Betrayal can occur in personal relationships, friendships, workplaces, or larger social or political contexts, and it frequently leads to feelings of hurt, anger, and loss.

Dishonor:

Dishonor is the loss or lack of respect, reputation, or integrity due to actions or behaviors that go against moral, ethical, or societal standards. It reflects a failure to uphold principles of honesty, loyalty, or responsibility, leading to shame, disgrace, or a tarnished reputation.

In summary, dishonor is the result of actions that undermine Trust, respect, or integrity. While it can cause significant personal and social harm, it is possible to restore honor through accountability, amends, and a commitment to ethical behavior moving forward.

Wickedness:

Wickedness is the deliberate act of doing wrong, harming others, or behaving immorally in ways that violate ethical, moral, or societal standards. It often involves malicious intent, selfishness, and a disregard for the well-being or rights of others.

Wickedness reflects a deeper level of wrongdoing, where actions are not only harmful but also driven by cruelty, dishonesty, or a corrupt mindset.

In summary, wickedness is the willful choice to act in ways that harm others and oppose what is good or right. It represents a profound moral failure that disrupts Trust, peace, and justice but can be countered through empathy, accountability, and moral courage.

Immorality:

Immorality refers to actions, behaviors, or attitudes that go against moral principles, ethical standards, or societal norms of what is considered right or good. It involves disregarding what is just, fair, or virtuous, often resulting in harm to oneself, others, or the community. Immorality can manifest in many forms, such as dishonesty, cruelty, exploitation, or indulgence in harmful behaviors.

In summary, immorality is the rejection or neglect of ethical and moral standards, often leading to harm or injustice. It is destructive to individuals and society, but it can be addressed through education, empathy, and a commitment to integrity and accountability.

Pt. 4 Chapter 4
The Value Chain

The Value Chain

A Service and/or A Product for Sale

+

- Quality Products/Services
- Great Work-Ethic
- Reasonable Prices
- Doing Good Business (Integrity)
- Consistency
- "Adaptivity"
- Prioritize the Generated Income/Revenue
- Good Communication
  - Explicit/Clear Communication
  - Proactive Communication
  - Transparent & Accountable Communication
  - Trustworthy & Dependable Communication

Clientele
- Statisfied Customers
- Repeat Customers
- Referred Customers

= Income/Revenue & Recurring Income/Revenue

A Quality Service or Product:

A quality product or service provided by a business can be described as one that

consistently meets or exceeds customer expectations in terms of performance, reliability,

value, and overall experience.

It reflects the business's commitment to excellence, attention to detail, and understanding of customer needs.

A quality product or service embodies reliability, value, and customer-centric design.

It stands out because it consistently delights customers, solves their problems,

and creates lasting satisfaction, which drives trust and loyalty for the business.

GREAT WORK-ETHIC

A great work ethic is characterized by a strong commitment to excellence, discipline, and integrity in one's work.

It reflects a person's attitude, values, and behaviors that consistently

demonstrate a dedication to achieving goals and maintaining high standards.

Traits of a great work ethic include:

-Punctuality: Always showing up on time and ready to work.

-Reliability: Following through on commitments and consistently delivering quality work.

-Initiative: Taking action and going above and beyond without being asked.

- Resilience: Staying focused and motivated even in challenging situations.

- Attention to Detail: Ensuring accuracy and care in all tasks.

- Positive Attitude: Maintaining enthusiasm and professionalism, even under pressure.

People with a great work ethic often inspire trust and respect from colleagues and leaders.

Consistency:

Consistency is the ability to repeatedly deliver dependable, high-quality results or actions over time.

In business, it means maintaining reliability in operations, products, services, and communication to regularly meet or exceed customer expectations.

Consistency is essential for survival in business because it builds trust, reinforces

your brand, ensures efficient operations, and creates a stable foundation for growth.

By maintaining reliability and steady performance, your business can adapt

to challenges, retain customers, and thrive in a competitive market.

Reasonable Prices:

Reasonable prices are good for business because they strike a balance between

profitability and customer satisfaction, fostering trust, loyalty, and long-term growth. Here's why:

Reasonable pricing makes products or services accessible

to a broader audience, encouraging more people to buy.

1. Attracts More Customers

2. Builds Trust and Loyalty

3. Enhances Market Position

- This strategy can strengthen your reputation in a competitive market.

4. Encourages Volume Sales

5. Reduces Customer Complaints

6. Increases Long-Term Profitability

-While higher prices may generate short-term gains, reasonable pricing

encourages sustained business growth by retaining customers.

- Repeat customers cost less to acquire than new ones.
- Loyal customers tend to spend more over time, boosting lifetime value.

7. Supports Economic Stability

-Reasonable prices contribute to the economic well-being of the

community by ensuring affordability for a diverse customer base.

- Businesses that serve their communities effectively often receive support in return.

8. Encourages Referrals and Word-of-Mouth

Customers are more likely to recommend businesses that offer fair value.

- Positive recommendations attract new customers.

- Reasonable prices are often cited in glowing reviews, amplifying your brand's reach.

Conclusion:

Reasonable pricing benefits businesses by attracting and retaining customers, fostering trust, and ensuring long-term profitability.

It strikes the right balance between customer satisfaction and business sustainability, making it a smart strategy for growth.

Adaptivity

Adaptivity is the ability to adjust, evolve, and respond effectively to changing conditions, environments, or demands.

It is a dynamic quality that allows businesses, systems, or individuals to modify their strategies,

behaviors, or operations to remain competitive and relevant in the face of uncertainty or challenges.

Why Adaptivity is Good for Survival in Business

1. It Keeps You Relevant in a Changing Market

2. It helps you respond to Competition

3. It helps you improve resilience During Crises

- Unforeseen disruptions like economic downturns, pandemics, or supply chain issues require quick adjustments.

- Businesses that adapt quickly can survive and even thrive during tough times.

4. It Encourages Innovation

- Adaptivity fosters a mindset of continuous improvement and creativity,

helping businesses develop new ideas and seize opportunities.

5. It Enhances Team Agility (the power of moving quickly and easily

8. It Supports Long-Term Growth

- Businesses that adapt continually find new growth opportunities and revenue streams.

- Adaptivity positions you to take advantage of emerging trends before competitors do.

How to Cultivate Adaptivity in Business

-Monitor Trends:

Stay informed about industry changes, customer preferences, and technological advancements.

Encourage Innovation:

Foster a culture that rewards creativity and problem-solving.

Be Agile:

Implement flexible systems and processes that allow quick changes.

Listen to Feedback:

Use customer and employee insights to guide your adaptations.

Invest in Learning:

Provide opportunities for professional development to help your team adapt to new challenges.

Conclusion:

Adaptivity is essential for business survival and success because it enables you to navigate change, innovate, and remain competitive. Your business can thrive in any environment by embracing a mindset of flexibility

and continuous improvement.

Prioritizing the Generated Income/Revenue:

Prioritizing your money in regard to running a business involves strategically allocating/distributing financial resources

to ensure the company's operations, growth, and profitability while maintaining financial health.

It requires careful planning, decision-making, and monitoring to balance immediate needs with long-term goals.

Key Aspects of Prioritizing Money in Business.

1. Covering Essentials First

- Prioritize operational expenses such as rent, utilities, payroll, and inventory.

- Ensure critical costs that keep the business running are paid on time.

2. Investing in Growth

- Allocate/distribute resources for marketing, advertising, and sales efforts to expand customer reach.

- Invest in technology, equipment, or staff training that improves efficiency and scalability.

3. Building a Financial Cushion

- Maintain a reserve or emergency fund to manage unexpected challenges like economic downturns or equipment failures.

- Avoid running the business paycheck-to-paycheck.

4. Managing Debt

- Prioritize paying down high-interest debts to free up cash flow.

- Consider reinvesting profits rather than relying heavily on borrowing for growth.

5. Profit vs. Reinvestment

- Decide how much profit to reinvest into the business (e.g., expanding operations,

product development) versus taking out for personal income or shareholder dividends.

6. Monitoring Cash Flow

- Focus on ensuring that inflows (revenue) exceed outflows (expenses) consistently.

- Use tools like cash flow projections to anticipate and plan for lean periods.

7. Customer Acquisition and Retention (Acquiring & Retaining Customers)

- Prioritize spending on strategies that attract new customers

and retain existing ones, as these directly impact revenue.

- Balance spending between acquisition (marketing) and retention (customer service, loyalty programs).

8. Compliance and Risk Management

- Set aside funds for taxes, licenses, and legal compliance to avoid penalties.

- Invest in business insurance and risk management tools to protect assets.

9. Data-Driven Decision Making

- Regularly review financial reports to assess the return on investment (ROI) for various expenditures.

- Redirect funds from low-performing areas to high-impact initiatives.

10. Scaling Gradually

- Avoid overextending resources by trying to grow too quickly.

- Prioritize sustainable growth over aggressive expansion.

Why It's Important:

Prioritizing money in a business ensures:

- Stability in operations.

- Efficient use of resources.

- Long-term growth and profitability.

- The ability to adapt to changing market conditions.

(((GOOD COMMUNICATION)))

CLEAR & EXPLICIT COMMUNICATION:

Clear communication ensures that the message is direct and unambiguous, leaving no room for misinterpretation.

Explicit communication focuses on being specific and detailed, stating everything

plainly without relying on assumptions or implied meanings.

Both terms emphasize precision and transparency, ensuring that all parties understand the message fully.

PROACTIVE COMMUNICATION:

Proactive Communication involves informing someone ahead of time about a potential

issue, such as being late, before it becomes a problem.

It shows responsibility and foresight.

TRANSPARENT & ACCOUNTABLE COMMUNICATION:

Transparent communication involves being open and honest about mistakes, ensuring the client knows the truth.

Accountable communication reflects taking responsibility for the error and addressing it

directly with the client, showing integrity and a commitment to making things right.

Both terms capture the professionalism and courage required in such situations.

TRUSTWORTHY & DEPENDABLE COMMUNICATION:

Trustworthy communication reflects the integrity of following

through on what was promised, building confidence in your word.

Dependable communication emphasizes reliability and

consistency, ensuring others can count on you to meet your commitments.

These terms highlight the importance of keeping your word and maintaining credibility.

RELIABLE COMMUNICATION:

Reliable communication reflects consistency and dependability—saying what you'll do and doing it.

Integrity:

Integrity is the quality of being honest, ethical (upright), and consistent in your actions, decisions, and values, even when faced with challenges or pressures.

In business, integrity involves sticking to moral and ethical principles, treating customers, employees, and stakeholders fairly, and maintaining transparency and accountability.

Benefits of Having Integrity in Business

1. Builds Trust

Integrity fosters trust among customers, employees, and partners.

Businesses known for honesty and reliability are more likely to retain loyal customers and attract new ones.

Example:

A company that admits mistakes and takes responsibility demonstrates trustworthiness.

2. Strengthens Reputation

A reputation for integrity enhances credibility and respect in the marketplace.

Businesses with strong ethical (honorable) standards often stand out as leaders in their industries.

Example:

Ethical (righteous) business practices can result in positive word-of-mouth and media coverage.

3. Encourages Customer Loyalty

Customers prefer doing business with companies they perceive as fair and honest.

Integrity in pricing, marketing, and service builds long-term relationships.

Example:

Transparent return policies and honest advertising strengthen customer loyalty.

4. Fosters a Positive Work Environment

Integrity at the leadership level sets the tone for company culture.

Employees are more engaged and motivated when they feel valued, respected, and treated fairly.

Example:

A company that promotes transparency and fairness is likely to attract and retain top talent.

5. Minimizes Risk

Businesses with integrity are less likely to face legal issues, scandals, or financial losses stemming from unethical (immoral) practices.

Ethical (moral) behavior reduces the risk of damage to reputation and financial penalties.

Example:

Avoiding deceptive practices helps a company steer clear of lawsuits or regulatory actions.

6. Promotes Long-Term Success

Integrity ensures that decisions are made with sustainability and fairness in mind, leading to steady growth.

It attracts like-minded investors, partners, and customers who value ethical (honest) practices.

Example:

Ethical supply chains build lasting partnerships and brand resilience.

7. Enhances Employee Morale and Productivity

Employees are more likely to respect and support leaders who act with integrity.

A fair and honest workplace culture fosters collaboration, creativity, and productivity.

Example:

Leaders who consistently practice what they preach inspire loyalty and dedication from their teams.

8. Builds Resilience in Crisis

During difficult times, businesses with integrity are more likely to maintain customer and stakeholder support.

Ethical (Fair & Moral) decision-making helps a company navigate crises without compromising its values.

Example:

A transparent response to supply chain delays earns customer understanding and patience.

Examples of Integrity in Business

*Honoring warranties and return policies without hidden terms.

*Being transparent about product limitations or risks.

* Paying employees and suppliers fairly and on time.

* Avoid deceptive marketing practices.

*Taking responsibility for mistakes and actively working to resolve them.

Conclusion:

Integrity is a cornerstone of sustainable success in business. It builds trust, loyalty, and a positive reputation while fostering a culture of accountability and fairness.

Businesses that operate with integrity are more likely to achieve long-term profitability and resilience as they attract loyal customers, dedicated employees, and supportive partners.

CLIENTELE:

A Satisfied Customer:

Is a customer that's subject to come back and SPEND "MONEY" again.

Repeat Customers:

Are customers that actually comes back and SPEND "MONEY" again!

Referred Customers:

A customer referred by another customer as a "Referred Customer".

This is how you create clientele!

Income/Revenue:

The Income/Revenue is the "MONEY" that's generated from Providing a Service or Selling a Product.

Recurring Income/Revenue:

The Income/Revenue from loyal, long-term, and committed customers is often described as "Recurring Income/Revenue."

[The End]
Conclusion

"Ignorance is a DISEASE"

&

"Stuck On Stupid is a Symptom of the DISEASE"

Conclusion

Life, at times, may feel overwhelming, unpredictable, and full of obstacles. But the truth is, this game of life is manageable—and anything you desire to achieve is within your reach. Success is not reserved for a select few; it is built by those who understand the importance of discipline, character, and the right mindset.

Sometimes, the only thing standing between where we are and where we want to be is the right ingredients—principles that guide us, habits that shape us, and wisdom that keeps us grounded. My hope is that this book has served as a valuable resource along your personal journey, providing insight, direction, and clarity as you work toward your goals.

I pray that within these pages, you have discovered timeless jewels—principles that will not only benefit you but also those who come after you. True generational wealth is not just in what we leave behind, but in who we become and what we instill in others.

And as you move forward, always remember: no one is stopping you but you. No one can exercise these principles for you—only you can put them into action. Your growth, your success, and your legacy are in your hands. You are in control of your own journey.

Thank you for being open to the knowledge, reflections, and insights within this book. May it serve as a stepping stone on your path to success, prosperity, and a life built on purpose.

Keep pushing forward. The journey continues.

It's All Luvvv

Game Element	Definition	Real-Life Equivalent
Participants	The players involved in the game	Everyday people like you and
Objective	The goal to win, score, or accomplish something	Achieve success, build wealth leave legacy
Rules	The guidelines and boundaries that must be followed	Laws, societal norms, cultural expectations
Rule Enforcers	Those who govern and ensure fair play	Police, judges, lawyers, government staff
Rule Makers	Those who create the rules and structure of the game	Politicians, lawmakers, system architects
Playing Field	The environment where the game unfolds	Society, community, economy
Time Clock	The limit or pacing of the game	Your lifespan, deadlines, time management
Scorekeeping	How progress is measured	Income, impact, results, goals achieved
Penalties	Consequences for breaking rules	Jail, fines, setbacks, lost opportunities
Opposition	Challenges or forces that test the players	Life's obstacles, competition, systemic barriers
Strategy & Growth	The skills and mindset needed to advance	Character development, knowledge, wisdom, mental maturity

ABOUT THE AUTHOR

Gregory Red, also known as Professor Gee, is a self-taught student of life, business, and personal growth. Born in New Orleans, he grew up in a world where the odds were stacked against people like him—and yet, through grit, humility, discipline, and the grace of God, he began rewriting his own narrative.

Through years of independent study and real-world experience, Gregory developed not only an understanding of financial literacy but also a deeper truth: "money is a tool, but character is the foundation." The urge to relay that understanding became the heartbeat of his mission to serve the people.

He's the founder of seeyourdollar.com, a free platform designed to teach financial literacy to underserved communities—breaking down complex money topics into practical, everyday lessons. While the website focuses on the numbers, this book focuses on the values behind the wealth.

Generational Wealth: Rich From the Inside Out is Gregory's way of giving direction to those who are trying to figure life out—especially those who come from the same type of environment he did. His message is simple: "if we pass down the right principles, the wealth will follow."

Learn more at seeyourdollar.com

www.ingramcontent.com/pod-product-compliance
Lightning Source LLC
Chambersburg PA
CBHW042259090526
44582CB00005B/114